ANOTHER NE
CHARLES S. L
HAS WRITTEN ... _____ OF IT ALL

    Beginning with his insertion onto Go Noi Island as a replacement for a wounded Company L machine gunner, and culminating with the healing Vietnam Veterans' Parade in downtown Chicago 18 years later, Chuck Lofrano has written intimately of his experiences, feelings and his new - found awareness of life around him. Published by Book Surge Publishing, the book is available for purchase at www.amazon.com

    A "must read" for all Marines, this literary work goes beyond Chuck's short stay with Lima Co. and his further service with the 7th Marines. It delves deeply into the author's psyche and his all important "attitude" about his personal life, his Corps, and his country.

Terry Rigney
Web Host for Official Marine 3/27 Web Site.
Author

SOME READERS REVIEWS:

"An amazing book. Tears of laughter and sorrow came very easily. Quite touching at times. I did not want the book to end. It must have been quite difficult to complete. Thanks to all those who serve our country."

"A real triumph! Great validation for those who serve our country. I could not put it down. Spielberg and Hanks should definitely take a look at it. I smell a movie deal."

"Quite engrossing and amazing to read about for one who was born a year after your tour of duty. I definitely recommend this book."

"Your book brought me tears, memories of those time and why war is so cruel but yet sometimes necessary. As we come to our Independence Day, I will have a more profound respect for all veterans."

"You've certainly lived an incredible life and I feel fortunate to have had the opportunity to have a peek into your perspective on our shared history as Americans.

…………I frequently had tears in my eyes when reading such statements as. 'I was reborn in that moment and I knew I would never be the same again', …..doubly so as I reached the story's end.

"Your book has certainly caught my attention, opened my eyes, taught me a thing or two and yes entertained me. All the things a good book should do. I am going back to amazon.com to get another copy of the book for a friend of mine who served in Vietnam."

'Reading had always taken me away from the rat race we live in. It forces me to use my imagination. Your book certainly did that."

"My father was in WWII. He said he saw his buddies being hurt and killed and didn't want to talk about it. I knew it was a bad time. I knew he didn't want me or my mom to know what happened. Thank you for some understanding of this."

INTRODUCTION

On March 17, 2003 feeling tired and weak, I went to see my doctor. After an examination and some tests he ordered me to go to the hospital. Two hours later and about four hours before I would have died I found myself in the ICU hooked up to a hemo dialysis machine. I was diagnosed with multiple organ shut down including the loss of my kidney function. I needed immediate care and would be on dialysis for the next three and a half years. During that time I had four serious heart attacks. One of these attacks, which was particularly severe, caused me to spend eight days on life support machines and medications culminating in quadruple by-pass surgery. The renowned doctor who performed the operation told my family that mine was the toughest surgery he had performed in his twenty-five years of experience.

Some friends and family members offered to donate a kidney but none were good matches. I did get a call late one Sunday night from Northwestern Memorial Hospital in Chicago. They had a cadaver kidney that was compatible. Unfortunately I was experiencing an infection at the time and was not able to take advantage of this life saving offer. Not until we had waited the recommended year after pregnancy when my daughter Lisa gave birth to my granddaughter Lizzie did I finally receive a perfect match. Even though Lisa's kidney was found to be compatible, I suffered frequent infections and heart trouble causing the transplant operation to be continually postponed. In addition, because of my heart condition, I was told the odds of surviving the transplant were only about forty percent. It was during this time that I began to reflect on my life. I had gone through hard times before. While fighting with the marines in Vietnam in 1968 as an Infantry machine gunner I received a disabling wound which took me through years of pain, hospitals and rehabilitation. The most fascinating thing about my introspection was that instead of feeling sorrowful, I felt contentment. As I reflected on my life I reviewed the good as well as the bad and found the good to be overwhelming. Since I didn't know if or for how long I might be around I wanted to leave the lessons I learned about life to my children and grandchildren.

As I began to think of what I wanted to say I was forced to concentrate on those things in my life that I considered blessings. There were the obvious and most important things, falling in love with and marrying my wife, the births of my children and grandchildren. Beyond these things I found many more joys and accomplishments that far outweighed the tragedies I had endured. I found many answers I hoped would help my daughters and their children as they faced the hardships which were sure to present themselves. At the same time I realized I had lived through some very interesting times. The sixties were a tumultuous period to say the least. The years of the Cold War, the information technology revolution and current world affairs certainly qualified as such.

As I thought of what was going on in the world, I found an affinity with the young men and women who were risking their lives in the service of their country. This led me to reflect on a celebration that I, through a series of events, was privileged to be a part of. "The Chicago Vietnam Veterans Welcome Home Parade" on June 13, 1986.

My intentions in writing this book are as I stated. I do not wish to present myself as an extraordinary person or as a hero. I knew heroes. I served with heroes and believe me, I am no hero. I did not receive the Congressional Medal of Honor, Navy Cross or Silver Star. I was simply a U.S. Marine Corps Infantry machine gunner who fought in Vietnam, as thousands of others did, in some of the bloody battles of 1968. Nor is this a historical review of the war. There are others, more learned and better-equipped than I, who have written eloquently on the subject. In fact, I ask pardon of those historians if I get some of the facts, dates, places and events out of sequence. I did my best to portray the events mentioned here as accurately as possible. To a grunt, the war is viewed as what is happening directly in front of him. The big picture, the overall strategy, has little meaning to him. The parts of this book about my time in Vietnam are taken from my experiences and rendered in my point of view. Collaborating information was taken from the declassified "After Action Reports" I received from the U.S. Marine Corps History and Museum Division, the Department of Defense, and the Department of Veterans Affairs.

I reflected on how my life had been determined through my experiences in the war. The war was always with me. It dictated the way I thought and the decisions I made. I instinctively knew my experiences were not unique. I recognized that all combat veterans from all wars have a shared consciousness. I believe the parts of my story covering my wounds and my journey through hospitals, rehabilitation and re-entry into society are universal. I also discovered that war is not the only thing that greatly affects the lives of individuals. My kidney failure, heart attacks and surgeries have also forced me to find a way to overcome obstacles and to continue to search for the meaning and values of life, as well as to fight for the happiness and goodness that is ours to claim. Others with life-threatening illnesses have had to do the same.

To my children and grandchildren, I want you to know that: I love you and I hope you will benefit from these stories. Day to day, life will be up and down, but overall, it's a great and wonderful journey that can bring peace, love and contentment. The ultimate decisions affecting your happiness will be your own.

To my brothers and sisters of all wars, I say: never let your detractors define you. Don't let people get away with saying they "honor the warrior but not the war." Don't be seduced by this although you may be tempted to do so in order to gain their support and sympathy. Think about what they are really saying. By dishonoring the war, what message are they sending? What are they saying to wounded and maimed soldiers or to the parents, spouses and children of those killed? The message is clear. They're telling them their loved ones were dupes who answered the call of our country to fight. They are to be viewed at best as victims and at worst as suckers. Remember that some of our troops from Vietnam who wanted to be accepted by certain segments of society negated their experiences. They spoke out against their brothers, even as a few Afghan and Iraqi veterans are doing now.

To those of you who have answered the call in times of danger, I ask you to hold your head high. Your mission in defense of freedom is noble and your unselfish sacrifices are pure. The lessons you have learned and the miseries you have overcome have made you stronger. Help teach others the importance of life and the trivialities of non-important matters.

"No greater love has man than that man lay down his life for another. "John, Chapter 15, Verse" 13. You were prepared to lay down your life for your country and your fellow man. Yours is the "Greater Love."

Welcome Home

*The day dawns bright on the Ville below
And through the ranks the word comes,
"Go. Stay on line, don't push too fast. It
makes no difference if you're first or last
for in this war where bullets fly, anyplace
you stand is a good place to die."*

*So whispers the sergeant as you slowly
walk down from the top of the hill to
the gates of the town. But what of the
civilians left inside? What of those with
no place to hide? they couldn't leave
as they were told so perish the young,
infirm and old.*

*Bullets have no time to debate to which
person they will direct their hate. Then
all of a sudden the air comes alive with
whizzes and zings like maddened bees
from a hive. No time to think of other's
strife the problem at hand is to preserve
your own life.*

*When the bees first stung, Mac went
down clutching his chest and cursing the
town. Off to the right four figures rear. A
burst from a '60 and they disappear. As
you pass through the gates, the worst
of your dreams, explosions and blood
and nightmarish screams.*

*Fear and excitement mingle inside.
Some laugh, some cry, some take it in
stride. Yesterday's cowards are heroes*

this day. Those who cursed God now start to pray. The staccato of gunfire is constant and loud. It cuts through them all, the Few and the Proud.

A century later the word is spread. "Cease fire, regroup, and count the dead." Can children of God cause these pains? These broken bodies and shattered brains? These things and more I chose to bear. My gift of freedom for all to share.

And if again my country would call, I'd go to her now in Spite of it All.

Charles S. Lofrano

CHAPTER ONE

Welcome to the "Nam"

South Vietnam
1968

The door of the commercial Continental jet airplane swung open. As I stood in the hatch I was physically taken aback as the essence of South Vietnam rushed over me with an oppressive onslaught of tropical heat. Strange exotic aromas that would take me some time to be able to recognize assaulted my senses together with the permeating smell of jet fuel. The flight from Okinawa to Da Nang had been surreal. The passengers had all been young marines dressed in green stateside utilities. The stewardesses were young, attractive women who volunteered for these somewhat harrowing flights. The Da Nang airfield was not immune to being shelled and the pilots had to undertake evasive maneuvers as they made their approach for landing. The banter on the flight was pretty much what you might imagine. We asked for kisses and other small privileges from these pretty girls, reminding them jokingly that this may be our last day on earth. They took it all in good humor and stayed to talk with us, steering us away from our crude comments and engaging us instead in conversations about where we were from and our girls back home. This last question always prompted a G.I. to reach in his wallet, display a picture and, if you didn't stop him, to go on forever about the beauty and virtue of the girl he left behind. I wondered if these women had been specially trained. They put us at ease at a time when we were filled with anxiety and fear. They saw to it that no one crossed the line, while still being pleasant and just a little bit flirtatious. As we deplaned some of them gave us a light kiss on the check and wished us good luck. A few of them had tears in their eyes; I was struck by this display of genuine concern.

We had spent several weeks at Camp Hansen on Okinawa prior to our leaving for Vietnam. We were given more training in jungle warfare as well as some time to help us adapt to the heat. Part of the training had been to walk through a jungle path nicknamed "The Ho Chi Minh Trail". Booby traps and obstacles were hidden on the path by the instructors. Ambushes were set up along the way to surprise us. The idea was obviously to avoid the booby traps, to discover the ambushes before they were sprung and to successfully negotiate the course. I had walked down the simulated Ho Chi Minh Trail five times and had been "killed" five times. I thought of this as I left the plane, quickly walked across the tarmac to the terminal, noticing several recently made bomb craters as I walked. Once inside the terminal we were directed to a line where we stood waiting to present our orders and to receive our instructions.

The terminal was filled with men at what seemed to be all stages of their tours. There were newly inserted troops who for the most part were still wearing stateside utilities. (I had taken some jungle utilities while on a detail in Okinawa. The detail was separating the clothing that had been removed from those who had been killed or wounded). There were men dressed in clean uniforms that were either leaving for or returning from R&R. Finally, there were those who I could tell were going home. Many of them looked gaunt and underfed. Some of them, most definitely grunts, were dressed in ill-fitting tropical uniforms devoid of rank, insignia or belts. They looked like someone had dressed them in a hurry from a pile of clothes that had no relation to what sizes were needed. I noticed that their attitude and walk had no correlation to the skeletal appearance of their faces. Their hollow eyes were filled with an unknowable understanding and a triumph that was impenetrable to one who had not had their experience. At the same time they walked with a swagger and a self-confidence. They seemed to be saying, "I made it! I survived." As their gazes engaged ours it was as if they looked through us and didn't see us at all. Later on, when I was one of them, I realized that they had seen us but didn't want to exchange glances because of the fear that we may be able to read their minds and run screaming back to the plane.

I presented my orders for verification and they were handed back to me. I was then told to wait outside in a specific area and that someone would be along shortly to pick me up. As I sat waiting alone, the reality of the situation continued to come over me in a wave. The whine of the Phantom Jets as they revved their engines in anticipation of takeoff was ear-shattering. The Jets came in to refill and rearm. They then took off for fire missions somewhere in the distance. Sometimes I could actually see them release their payloads and witness the smoke raised by their ordinance. A few times I heard the explosions, which sounded like distant thunder. When several bombs were dropped simultaneously, there was a rumbling that built to a crescendo of perceived power and devastation. I could also hear the crackle of small arms fire but couldn't tell how close it was. The movement of planes, men and equipment, and the display of violence in the outlying countryside snapped me into the reality of the situation

I was in a war. I was about to join a fighting unit and my main objective was to seek out other men to kill. I was filled with a combination of fear, youthful bravado, and sheer awe at the tableau surrounding me. Nothing in my background or training could have prepared me for this, let alone for what was to come in the following days. For a fleeting moment I thought, "Wow, I really fucked up!" Luckily I suppressed that emotion and replaced it with a firm resolve to do my best and to fulfill my duty and commitment to my country, to my Marine Corps, and to myself. This affirmation didn't totally calm my fears, but it helped to push them down inside. I would use this method later on when fear and hardship entered my life.

As I became acclimated, though not accustomed, to the bustling activity around me and the evidence of violence in the distance, I started to focus on the countryside. Immediately around the airfield was sand. There was a clean line of sight all around which made it more difficult to understand how the airfield was being mortared and shelled. In the distance I could see rugged mountain ranges. Between the area around the airfield and the mountains were green rice paddies. I knew that thick, canopied jungles lay out ahead and in between the mountains, and I was struck by the contradicting terrain and breathtaking beauty of this war-torn country.

My thoughts were interrupted by a sergeant who was walking towards me. He told me that my transportation had been delayed and that I would have to wait until morning to be picked up. My orders read that I was to be a line replacement for the 3rd Battalion, 27th Regiment, 1st Marine Division. I knew the 27th had been hit pretty hard in the beginning of the Tet Offensive and was in need of replacements. On the way to my temporary barracks the sergeant explained that the 27th was once again engaged in an operation. He said this was all he could tell me but he was sure I would be briefed when I was picked up in the morning. His words caused a panic in my mind. I don't know what had made me think I would be gradually entered into combat but I certainly wasn't prepared to start my war tomorrow. I tried to rationalize that since I was new and untested, I would be held back from the fighting until I was ready. Even though the Regiment was involved in an operation, surely there was a base where the support and administration personnel were stationed. I failed to allow myself to face the fact that those in support and administration at base camp were there because that was their job. My job was as an infantry machine gunner and if the shit was hitting the fan somewhere it was my duty to go there and help try to stop it.

I barely slept that evening. The stillness of the night was frequently interrupted by the gunfire and explosions in the distance. I had been instructed that the 1st Marine Division landed in Vietnam in 1965 and was stationed in I Corps. South Vietnam had been divided into four sections.*

Of course I didn't know these particulars at that time. I lived through it and experienced it first hand, but a grunt's view of war is limited to what is going on directly in front of him. I had also yet to learn the other enemies I would be fighting and experiencing in I Corps: the heat and monsoons, the triple canopied jungles, rugged mountains, and hot sandy terrain.

That first night all I could think about was what tomorrow would bring. How would I perform? Would I be brave or would I be a coward? I felt prepared and I felt hard. My Marine Corps training had given me that but I still felt the constraints of civilization that resisted the violence I knew was to come. I was positive all my brothers in all wars went through the same dichotomy. War is an atypical situation, to say the least. Most people who have not faced combat have no idea of the tremendous conflict within the soul of those who face it. There are those who are quick to claim that we who fight are too stupid to have any feelings about what we are expected to do. They dismiss us as bloodthirsty killers who enjoy killing women and children. Negating the mental as well as physical sacrifices we make gives them moral superiority. They declare that it's only the dumb, psychotic, bloodthirsty poor with no other options in life who would actually fight and put such a concept as freedom ahead of their own self-centered lives. The enlightened, privileged and elite Brahmins must be spared and protected so they could think great thoughts and tell the rest of us how to live. It was not enough to disagree with us. They had to destroy our motives, sacrifices and us personally in order to conceal their cowardice. This was a successful tactic that followed us for years after the war ended.

*They were called First, Second, Third and Fourth Corps. They subsequently became known as I Corps, II Corps, III Corps and IV Corps. I Corps consisted of the five provinces of Quong Nhi, Quong Tin, Quang Nam, Thua Thien and Quang Tri and was in the northernmost section of South Vietnam. The Ben Hai River separated North and South Vietnam to form the DMZ (Demilitarized Zone). Almost half of all U.S. combat forces in Vietnam, thirty army and twenty-four Marine Corps maneuver battalions (front-line combat units), were concentrated in I Corps. Here, the North Vietnamese had also concentrated their striking power, close to fifty battalions. *After Tet: The Bloodiest Year in Vietnam* By Ronald H. Spector

The 1st Marine Division had a threefold mission: searching for and destroying the enemy, defending key airfields and lines of communications, and conducting a pacification development program. The division was responsible for over one thousand square miles and extended protection to more than one million Vietnamese. Most action in the I Corps Tactical Zone during August of 1968 was centered in the 1st Marine Division's TAOR (Tactical Area of Responsibility). The enemy was looking for a victory that would achieve some measure of psychological or propaganda value to coordinate with the demonstrators back home. They mounted an attack of major proportions against Da Nang but were thoroughly repulsed, sustaining heavy casualties. Taken from "The Presidential Unit Citation Presented to The First Marine Division(Reinforced), Fleet Marine Force For Extraordinary Heroism and Outstanding Performance of Duty in Action Against Enemy

Forces in The Republic of Vietnam From 16 September 1967 To October 1968."

That night I prayed to God that I would live through this and come home with all the parts that I had left it with. As I finally started to close my eyes I heard and felt a loud explosion which shook the ground. My eyes snapped open and I saw a large ball of orange-red fire in the distant sky to the north. The gates were opening and in a few hours I would be going through them, over the river, past the three-headed dog and into the kingdom of hell.

The heat was always the first thing I noticed in the morning. Whether it was 95 degrees or 105 it weighed me down and seemed to sap my strength. After I got out of the shower I immediately started sweating again. If I had known this would be the last shower I would have for another three weeks, I'm sure I would have lingered in the water a lot longer. I spotted the six-by rolling toward me. I had been waiting since 4:30 AM for my ride. As I sat on the steps of the barracks I didn't know what mode of transportation would be sent for me, but when I saw the six-by I immediately knew it had come for me. It came to a halt, brakes screeching, and lurched forward. A marine jumped out of the driver's side walked up to me. He asked me if I was PFC Charles S. Lofrano. I stood transfixed as I took in this man standing before me. The first thing I noticed was that he was covered in red dust, as was the truck. From top to bottom he was the epitome of what I envisioned a marine warrior to look like. He was about my height, slender with a tanned, rugged complexion. On his head was a helmet with a green camouflage covering. Around the circumference of the helmet was a black band. Stuck inside the band was a pack of Kool cigarettes and a small clear bottle of bug repellent, which was called "bug juice." Around his neck were his taped-together dog tags and also what was called a "John Wayne Can Opener." This was a small device used to open C-Rations. He wore a green jungle utility shirt over which was web gear from which hung hand grenades. On his web belt were four canteens, a .45 caliber automatic pistol, a K-Bar (Survivor Knife) and a pouch containing ammunition. Strapped over his shoulder to his hip was a belt of 7.62 M60 machine gun rounds. He had green jungle utility trousers with large side pockets that were bloused over his green jungle boots. Quickly taking this all in at a glance, I was drawn to his eyes. Although his face was dirty and covered with red dust, his eyes were clear and steady. As I looked into them I realized that he knew things that I did not know, but that I was soon to find out.

    This all happened in an instant and I finally heard myself saying that yes, I was PFC Lofrano. The marine stuck out his hand declared that he was Staff Sergeant Mason, Weapons Platoon

Sergeant, Lima Company, 3rd Battalion, 27th Marines. As he shook my hand he stared me straight in the eyes and said, "Welcome to the 'Nam'". I looked deep into his eyes to see if there was any subterfuge or mockery in his statement. I could find none. Instead I detected a strong sense of concern and compassion, which made me immediately like this seasoned warrior.

Telling me to grab my gear, Sergeant Mason led me to the back of the truck. He held my things for me as I jumped on to the bed. He turned to get back inside the six-by as I arranged myself on the bench that was attached to the side. While getting behind the wheel, he stretched his neck out of the window and called back for me to face outboard, warning me to hold on to my seat. With that, he started forward and I soon learned the meaning of his warning. It was difficult to stay in my seat as the truck rolled over the pockmarked road. Several times I was lifted off the bench as we traveled over ruts and bumps of this unpaved highway.

While I was being jostled about I started noticing the change in the landscape from sandy, barren soil to villages surrounded by green rice paddies. I could see water buffaloes pulling crude plows, some ridden by small children urging them on by swatting them with long slim bamboo switches. As I looked out at the scene around me, I was struck by the timelessness it portrayed. I imagined that these people were living as they no doubt had lived a thousand years ago. I knew cities like Da Nang and Saigon were more westernized, and that there was a long history of European influence in most of the main cities. In fact, most people in urban areas spoke fluent French. Out here in the countryside I could sense that life was as it had always been.

As we passed by the villages I noticed that some of the people lifted their heads to look at us, but most ignored us. They continued to work, calf deep in the water of the rice paddies, pulling up the shoots, hoeing and planting. As I watched them I wondered what they were thinking. Did they see me as a liberator, as an occupier, or as a mere distraction in their lives? Later on when I was out even further away in the country, our chieu hoi scouts (enemy captives who defected to us and became our scouts and interpreters) would tell us that the NVA and Vietcong would tell the people lies about us to get them to rebel against us. One of the lies was that we were the French coming to take the land back. Another was that in order to become a United States Marine you had to kill your own mother and eat a live baby.

I wasn't sure where we were going.

I was told that the 27th was in the middle of a regimental size operation and I would be joining them there. I had been hoping that I would be given some time to become more acclimated with my new environment. I wasn't even supplied with the equipment I would need to enter combat. The marines were the last ones to receive M16 rifles. I had trained and qualified with the M14 and was told we would eventually be issued the M16s. Although my specialized training was with the M60 machine gun I couldn't expect to be a gunner right away. A gun team was made up of four marines whose jobs consisted of: a gun team leader/gunner, assistant gunner and two ammo-bearers. Odds were that I would be using an M16 before I got to be a gunner. The point was that I didn't have an M16 nor was I trained with one.

    The beginning of the Tet Offensive earlier that year had changed and sped up the planning process, proving once again that the enemy often disrupts the best-conceived strategies with actions of their own and that you go to war with the best army you have. I hadn't yet learned not to worry about things I had no control over. "The Green Machine" had it all covered

    I could see the base camp in the distance. Its details became more clear as we approached. The camp was surrounded by a sand berm topped with barbed wire. Inside the berm were a series of Quonset huts and wooden billets. Wooden towers were spaced around, up against the berm facing outbound. In the towers on either side of the gate were fifty- caliber machine guns. Concertina barbed wire was strung outside the berm around the entire perimeter. Metal cans and lids hung loosely from the razor-sharp wire These would give an early warning if someone were trying to go through the wire toward the camp during the night.

Once inside I was told that in addition to the wire, booby traps and claymores were placed and changed periodically so the enemy would not know where they might be. The entrance to the field of barbed wire and booby traps was a gate flanked by sandbagged machine gun emplacements. As we came to the gate, four marines came from the gun emplacements. Two approached the truck and two stood by with weapons at the ready. Sergeant Mason gave a password and handed some papers to the marine who was holding out his hand. The other marine walked to the passenger side, looked inside and then came around to the back to check me out. I nodded my head and gave him a slight smile as his eyes went over me. He didn't respond to my greeting and he never changed his expression. I sensed he didn't think too much of me and I felt diminished by his reaction. I should not have taken it personally. I learned later that there was a phrase for guys like me, just in from the world. The phrase was FNG (Fucking New Guy). This was a way, consciously or subconsciously, of not having to take the energy to learn the name or make an emotional contact with a guy who may be wounded and sent home or killed quickly. It was hard enough to endure the loss of those you did come to know. There was no need to add to that list if you could avoid it. The gate was opened and we rolled on toward the entrance to the berm. Once again we were stopped, inspected and passed through. I had the distinct feeling that this was the equivalent of a frontier fort in the middle of Indian country.

As the truck came to a stop, Sergeant Mason jumped out and came to help me off the back with my gear. We walked to a wooden hut and I noticed the words "3RD BN, 27TH REG HQ" stenciled in black on a red placard. There were several chairs placed around a small table in the outer room of the HQ. An administrative clerk came out and sat down with Sergeant Mason and me. The clerk had me fill out some forms, gave me some cursory instructions about mail and pay, and made sure I understood my life insurance options. When the clerk was finished with this procedure, he welcomed me and left us. Sergeant Mason then informed me of my immediate schedule

The regiment was currently in a place called Go Noi Island. They had fought a major battle there in mid-May and recently returned to clear the area once again so a major army base could be built there. Since this was in the TAOR of the 27th Marines, it was their job to accomplish this task. The 27th had run into a major NVA regiment and were now engaged in major combat which included tanks, air support, artillery battles and offshore bombardment by a naval battleship. Casualties were high and replacements were desperately needed. Sergeant Mason apologized and said that I would be joining one of his gun teams which was attached to the 3rd Platoon in about ten hours. Before I left he would walk me through the process of getting the supplies I needed. These would include an M16 rifle, ammunition, magazines to house the ammunition, canteens, web gear, poncho, rucksack, hand grenades, blanket, a mess kit, a bandolier to hold my magazines, an entrenching tool (foldable small shovel), shelter halves and pegs for erecting a tent, and a few days of C-Rations. He would then give me instructions on the firing and care of the M16 rifle that would include establishing my battle sights and also the ability to tear it down and reassemble it.

I had been told that while the M14 was built for minimal maintenance in all types of weather, its weight and design were prohibitive in the humid oppression of the jungle. The M16 was lighter and equipped with a dial that could immediately change the weapon from a semi automatic to fully automatic with a flip of a switch. The trade off was that the M16, with its lighter components, had a requirement of higher maintenance and had to be kept cleaner and drier. The introduction of the M16 caused a lot of controversy in its early introduction in Vietnam. Soldiers who had been used to the rugged characteristics of the M14 were not prepared for the more delicate mechanisms of the new rifle and many jams and misfires were reported early on.

By 7:00 that night I was on my way to Go Noi Island with Sergeant Mason. I had been issued my gear and snapped in with my M16. I was able to get only two canteens but was told I would be able to pick up more from the dead and wounded as they became available. The same was true with the magazines. My bandolier had space for seven twenty- round magazines but I had been issued only four. I had also been issued three hand grenades, a blanket that read "U.S. Army," and all the other items on my list.

A formation of three silver, sleek F-4 Phantom Jets flew like birds of prey over our heads as we approached what I believed to be our lines on Go Noi Island. We waited as they dropped their ordinance at what I thought to be an alarmingly close proximity to those lines. I didn't have to be a battle-hardened veteran to realize that this could only mean that the enemy was very close. I would soon be able to tell the difference between a five-hundred- and seven-hundred-fifty-pound bomb. It would become easy to identify the sight, color, and smell of napalm. Cluster bombs and Bouncing Bettys would become familiar to me.

At this time ,however, I looked in awe as a child looks at fireworks for the first time, mouth open with a mixture of excitement wonderment and fear.

After the air strikes we disembarked from the six-by. Weighted down as I was with the addition of the newly-acquired equipment, I made a somewhat clumsy approach to my new companions. It would take me awhile to properly balance this weight and move but for now let's just say that the memory of Fred Astaire's grace had nothing to fear from me. Third Platoon Lima had been pulled from the battle and Sergeant Mason had told me that this evening they were scheduled to set up a nighttime ambush. My gun team would be going with them.

A company of tanks had set up a defensive line and the members of the 3rd Platoon were lounging in various restful positions. I could feel them watching me as I walked toward them, trying not to stumble. Most of them were emotionless but I did notice some raised eyebrows and suppressed snickering. I could almost read their minds. "FNG," "Dufus," "Pogue" and "Useless" were just a few of the comments I psychically picked up. Sergeant Mason led me to three marines reclining around an M60 machine gun. One of them was brushing the 7.62 rounds still in the hundred-round belt with a toothbrush. He was periodically dipping the toothbrush into a bottle of LSA oil. Sergeant Mason introduced me to the team: Corporal Mullins (nicknamed "Moon"), the gun team leader and gunner, PFC "Whitey" (I never learned his real name) and PFC Johnson. Like me, Johnson was new in country. He was an ammo-bearer or "humper." I was told I was replacing Philly, who had been wounded and was being shipped back to the world. I would start my duties as an additional ammo-bearer.

On normal marches, in addition to my equipment, I would also be carrying two to four boxes of 100 rounds each of ammunition, depending on the expectations of the action. The hundred-round boxes were in a sling that was carried around the neck. On a normal patrol each of the two ammo-bearers and the assistant gunner would carry two hundred rounds. The gunner would have a hundred round belt worn like a bandolier and a fifty-round belt wrapped around his gun. I was told that some of the other grunts would be humping some rounds for us and overall we would normally go out with about a thousand rounds. I was naïve enough to think at the time that this was a lot of ammunition. By the time I got to be gunner I would demand a minimum of fifteen hundred to two thousand rounds.

As Whitey and Johnson tried to get some more sleep, Moon called me over to him. He asked me some basic questions and seemed to be satisfied with my personnel file, which Sergeant Mason had given him before he left us. He commented on the qualifications and scores I had gotten in boot camp, ITR (Infantry Training Regiment) and gun school. I got a sense that while these things were important to him, he was more interested in getting an idea of what kind of marine I was. Could he and his team count on me when the bullets started to fly? I knew what he was thinking because I was thinking the same thing. This was it. No more training. No backing out. I couldn't go home to my mother and ask her to tell these men that I couldn't go out to play. They had to rely on me, and I on them: not to accomplish a task, to make a key block in a championship game, or to get a clutch hit to break a tie. Tonight we would have to rely on one another to stay alive.

Moon told me that he had been in-country since November of '67. He was in Vietnam when Tet first broke out and had experienced the changes and escalation that occurred afterward. He had been wounded twice but not seriously enough to be sent home. He said that Allenbrook in May was pretty rough and that he hoped it would be better this time. Then, although I sensed he was only a few years older than I, he told me in what I felt was a fatherly tone to report to him before we shoved off. He wanted to make sure I was squared away and had what I needed for the mission. He noticed that I didn't have a flak jacket. This was no big deal for tonight, he said, but he would see that I had one tomorrow. I knew there was no quartermaster out here. I didn't have to ask Moon how he would provide me with one. I remembered what Sergeant Mason told me back at base camp when I was issued fewer canteens, magazines and hand grenades than I would need. He had said that I would be able to pick up more from the dead and wounded as they became available. The thought of this chilled me to the bone. Moon was telling me that there would be men killed and injured even tonight. My God! Would I be one of them?

I had no point of reference for this. My mind jumped to a different dimension. I felt that my entire life before this moment had no meaning. Everything I had ever worried about, stressed over, or been depressed about seemed small and insignificant. I was reborn in that moment. I knew that whatever happened, I would never be the same again.

Moon said that we would be forming up in a couple of hours. He suggested that I try to get some rest and then left. I collected my gear and laid down with my head propped on my rucksack. I couldn't remember what day of the week it was. I certainly couldn't remember my training. As I tried to calculate what the day was, I drew a complete blank. I started to panic but I knew there was no way I was going to ask any of my new comrades. I was sure I wasn't too high on the popularity chart and I didn't want to add to my lowly status by asking a foolish question. Moon came over to me during my mental consternation to give me halizone tablets and iodine pills. These were used to help purify the water and fight off bacteria. As Moon turned from me, I almost stopped him to ask what day of the week it was but I realized how peculiar this might be. It seemed strange that I was obsessed with the day of the week, but I realized later why it had been so important to me. If I were going to die, I would like to know what the date was.

Sometime during the night Moon came to gather the team. He told us we were to be attached to the first and second squads of 3rd Platoon. We would go out en masse, drop off a four-man radio team to set up an LP (Listening Post), and then would proceed about half a klick (kilometer) to a spot near the Thu Bon River. Moon went over my gear. He made sure I would be traveling as light as possible and still be prepared for contingencies. After his inspection, I was left with five magazines of twenty rounds each. In addition I had three hand grenades, one canteen, my M16 rifle, helmet and rucksack. Inside the rucksack were a blanket and two boxes of C-Rations. Slung over each of my shoulders was a box of M60 machine gun rounds. To this day, once in a while without warning, my mind snaps back to that first ambush and I can feel my heart begin to beat more rapidly.

As I waited for the command to shove off, I was filled with a combination of fear and excitement. I looked up and down the column to see if I could get a sense of what the other marines were thinking. There was no answer to be discerned as I found most visages to be almost blank and unreadable. I would come to know that it was better to try to empty the mind in order to remain focused. It was necessary to have a clear mind in order to respond to the stimuli which would be presented. However, at the time, it panicked me more that I was unable to find an answer in the faces of my peers. I needed to determine if I were the only one on the verge of a nervous breakdown.

The word came: "Lock and Load!" I heard a series of sharp metallic clicks as magazines were inserted into M16s, bolts were pulled back and released to drive rounds into the firing position, and safety catches were flipped off. I followed the order in the correct sequence, not realizing what I had done until it was over. The next command was, "Move out!" To my amazement, my feet reacted and I found myself moving out with the rest of the marines. By that time the night sky was lit only by moonlight. I had heard that the night belonged to the enemy, like a rival gang back in the world invading one's neighborhood. Enemy scouts could have been sent into the area previously, but they did not know the home turf as the residents did. Those who lived there knew the alleys, the hiding places, the short cuts, and the side streets. Locals knew the best places to jump an enemy and the best routes of escape if they were needed. Daytime gave us the advantage of air support, pin-point artillery and Huey Helicopter Gunships. At night we could still call in artillery and air support, but the accuracy was diminished.

As we headed toward the Thu Bon River, we came across a field of rice paddies. Around each rice paddy were dirt walls about four feet high which formed a rectangle keeping the water and rice shoots contained. After a healthy tropical rain, not to mention the Monsoons, the water in the paddies would rise and the top of the walls would become slick. In this field there was no discernible road. All the paddies were connected and the only way to traverse them was to walk on top of the paddy walls. Unfortunately these walls were wet and slippery on this night. My attempt to keep my balance on top of the slick walls resembled a comedy routine by Charlie Chaplin or Buster Keaton. I would take one step and slip. I'd get up, slip again, stumble and slip. I could hear derisive whispers from the rear telling me to keep moving or they'd shoot me off the wall, etc. I didn't believe that they would actually shoot me off the wall but I knew that I was jeopardizing all of our safety by making noise that might cause us to become exposed.

Just as I got the hang of keeping my balance by focusing and taking my time, we came to the end of the rice paddies. I was thankful for the darkness and hoped that because of it, no one would be able to recognize the clumsy FNG who had endangered the patrol.

Baptism by Fire

We set down in a copse of trees to rest and await orders. Lieutenant Sharp came over to pass the word to Moon and in the tradition of the service Moon passed the word down to us. G-2 (Intelligence) had identified major enemy activity in this area. If this corridor remained unchallenged, the enemy could bring in reinforcements and supplies to hit our positions on the right flank. If our ambush were successfully sprung, it would not be measured by the body count of the NVA. The fact that we had discovered their infiltration point was enough to close it off to them. They would know that our artillery and air support would be given these coordinates and could then be called down on them at any time.

We set up an "L" shaped ambush with first squad occupying the vertical line, and second squad occupying the horizontal line with our gun team connecting them. By the time we got settled it was almost completely dark. Most of the moonlight, which had assisted us in our march was now obscured by gathering clouds.

The marines of first squad laid out some trip wires and claymore mines, which, when engaged, would be the signal that the enemy had entered the killing zone of the ambush. On a night ambush no one spoke, smoked, or moved about. On these dark nights the imagination could go wild. Many a tree and bush became riddled with bullets by a young marine swearing that it was advancing toward him.

We were given one-hour watches each but there was no way I could get any sleep. In combat situations the body turns inside out. Nerves, adrenalin and senses are in a heightened state, taking precedence over thought. I had a feeling that I was experiencing the primeval survival instincts of our prehistoric ancestors. All the years of civilization are swept away and man is reduced to relying on pure animal instincts. This is where training and experience kick in. The training I had was the best. Unfortunately I drew a zero on the experience. I didn't know what to expect and hoped that my training and instincts would be enough to see me through my first firefight.

Moon gave me the first watch. I think he did this so he could secretly keep an eye on me. Sometime after my watch began I got a strange feeling that something was stirring. There had been some movement in the surrounding bushes but the marine on watch assured me that it was an animal. I was told that the NVA were not so stupid as to be that obvious but I still felt that something was not right. I didn't know if I was affected by the almost imperceptible tenseness of Whitey or the instant complete stillness suddenly around us.

Whatever the reason, my feelings were immediately validated by flares brightening the dark night sky followed by claymore explosions, shouts and gunfire. The flares revealed the outline of soldiers in full battle gear. This indicated that they were indeed NVA regulars and not VC (Viet Cong). As guerilla fighters the VC relied on hit and run tactics and the ability to hide amongst the people in the countryside. The NVA were hardcore troops that were well-trained and well-equipped. They were led by some of the same officers who had fought the French fifteen years earlier and the Japanese twelve years before that. They were taught small and large scale combat operations and, like us, they were also taught the best thing to do when ambushed was to charge the ambush instead of lying down and waiting to be killed. The Tet Offensive destroyed most of the Viet Cong infrastructure. Most of the fighting in South Vietnam by this time was conducted by the NVA. When the enemy was spotted the first question usually was, "Are they wearing uniforms?" If the answer was in the affirmative we knew we were in for a fight, and a fight was what we got that night.

    As soon as the flares went off the marines opened up a withering barrage of small arms fire. We could see a steady stream of red tracer rounds going out from our position to be immediately answered by green tracer rounds from the AK-47s of our adversaries. Moon jumped behind the M60 and started firing while Whitey fed the hundred-round belt into the gun. Johnson and I set up on each side of the gun and were told to pick our targets. The sights, sounds and smells before me were a surreal nightmare. The flares popping off in the night sky were giving off an artificial light. As the white phosphorous died down it left a black canvas of night on which was painted red and green bright lines coming in and out from the tracers. By this time our mortars started firing into the killing zone. The wump!, wump! from their tubes added to the gunfire, shouting and screams of men in pain. I had smelled cordite before in training but this was different. It mixed with the other smells of heat, humidity, vegetation and the sweet sickly smell of blood that I would experience many times again in this hell-spawned country. These sights, sounds and smells created a multi-sensory panorama that stays with me to this day.

Rounds were coming in, hitting the trees around us with sharp thuds. They made snapping sounds as they cut through the tall grass. Two of the enemy ran toward our position and Moon cut them down. He ordered me to throw a grenade at the fallen enemy on the ground to make sure they were dead. The rattle of gunfire was intense and accented by the explosions from our mortars. For half of the firefight my head was down as I tried to make myself small behind the fallen log I was using as cover. Every once in a while I would raise my rifle and fire in the direction of the enemy without seeing what I was shooting at.

Then, just as suddenly as it had started, the firing stopped. The NVA had made a rare, uncharacteristic mistake. They had walked into our ambush and been caught off guard. I knew we hadn't killed them all and I lay transfixed waiting for what was to happen next. Moon kept us in our positions and put Whitey behind the gun. He whispered that he was going over to second squad to see if he could figure out what was going on.

After a while he came back and told us we were to hold our position. We were to stay awake with all eyes on the alert. We were to remain still with no smoking and no talking. We were going to wait until it got light and then we would get the word. I looked at the sky and figured that we would not have to wait long.

At first light several marines from second squad slowly walked from their positions to the killing zone of the ambush. When I saw they had walked through the zone with no consequences I stood and stretched my cramped body. Johnson had already lit a blue heat tab and was boiling water to mix in the instant coffee and preparing his breakfast of C-Rations. I watched as our men policed the area and was amazed at what they found. The firefight had lasted for about forty-five minutes. The firing was intense and it seemed that nothing caught in the middle of that meat grinder could survive. Although they had seemed to be a reinforced company, the sweep had uncovered only seven bodies, including the two that lay in front of our position. How could this be? Our casualties were two dead and four wounded but we had been firing from heavy cover with the element of surprise. The enemy had gotten caught in the open, stayed their ground and pulled out sometime before dawn. Where were their wounded? How could we have killed only seven of them? Why were there so few pieces of their equipment left behind? I had heard stories about these wily, efficient, rock-hard NVA soldiers. I was starting to develop a deep respect for these committed warriors.

We marched back to our lines and I felt that I had experienced an entire lifetime in the last forty-eight hours. The men around me seemed to look at me differently. I knew I wasn't fully accepted yet but I felt the fact that I had survived a firefight and conducted myself responsibly was a beginning. How could I ever explain these things to my family and friends back home? Could I shatter their beliefs in man's humanity? Could I uncover to them the frailty of even the strongest of men? Could I tell my young friends of the razor-thin line between life and death, and if I could, how would I be able to explain to them the fierce pride I still felt in serving the country that I loved?

We must have infuriated the NVA by denying them their infiltration route at the river with our ambush. The next night they retaliated by hitting us with an intense barrage of artillery, mortars and rockets. I had just laid down in my fighting hole when an explosion shook the earth beside me and lifted me slightly off the ground. Most of the tanks that shielded our perimeter when I first arrived pulled out on a mission earlier in the day and left us with no cover. A firefight is a frightening ordeal, but being able to shoot back makes one feel he has some control in defending himself. Lying exposed to rockets and bombs falling on one's position is a much deeper level of hell. At night, it truly feels like the end of the world has arrived.

There were bright, white flashes of incandescent light, followed by ear-shattering explosions going off constantly. A steady rain of burning shrapnel was falling and I felt such an all consuming fear that I wanted to pull the earth over my head. I hoped I had built my fighting hole deep enough so the flying shrapnel would pass over me. There was no protection, however, from a direct hit. I lay there frozen like a horizontal statue. I didn't dare move or attempt to look out from my hole. Every once in a while between explosions I could hear yelling and screaming from our positions. This only added to the nightmarish feeling of the scene. I prayed to God and asked him to save me but if it was my time, to please make it quick. With that I resigned myself to accept whatever happened. I remember thinking at the height of the shelling that I just didn't care. Even death would have been welcomed as an end to this ordeal.

Our artillery batteries finally found the range. After a deafening salvo of outgoing rounds that created our own light show, the enemy's guns were silenced. I waited in my hole until the shelling from both sides stopped. I lifted my head from what I previously thought was going to be my grave. The night was humid and the residue of thick, slow rising gun smoke hung on the ground like a lingering fog. As I looked around I was amazed that the world was still standing. I don't know what I expected to see but, surprisingly, the landscape looked largely the same. Could nothing affect this war-scarred country? I felt I was in an episode of the *Twilight Zone* where the world would be destroyed each night only to have everything back to normal the next day.

Before arriving in Vietnam I had heard the story of the Battle of Khe Sahn. On January 21, 1968 forty thousand soldiers of the North Vietnamese Army (NVA) surrounded fifty-six hundred marines of the 26th Regiment and four hundred of their South Vietnamese allies. On the first day, the marines received three hundred rounds of incoming hostile rocket, mortar and artillery rounds. For the next seventy-seven days the NVA sent an average of one hundred and fifty shells per day into the camp. After my first night of being under such an attack I thought of those marines and believed their place in heaven was secured, because they already spent their time in hell.

By my third day in combat I had lived through an offensive ambush and survived a savage shelling. In both instances men were killed and wounded, but I had not a scratch. The question I kept asking myself was why. Was life this random? How could something so fragile be that meaningful? If it could end so abruptly what was the point? Which was real? Was it the life back in the world of comfort and self-indulgence, or was it this savage existence of kill and be killed? Was anything worth this? Since I could not come up with any answers I knew I had to bury these questions inside myself. To dwell on them would be suicide. I would need to clear my mind and do the best

I could to try to stay alive. A fatalistic feeling started to permeate my soul. It was the feeling that no matter how squared away I got, in the end, it would not be up to me whether I lived or died.

    A few days later those thoughts were further driven home. We were sitting down with second squad preparing a meal of C-Rations when Sergeant Mason came over to our area. He said the monsoons had washed two marines off a bridge about a half klick up the swollen river and he was asking for volunteers to look for them. A monsoon was a treacherous downpour of heavy rain and high winds that would start suddenly out of nowhere. The wind would drive the rain so fiercely I would swear it was coming horizontally. If we were dug in, the water would fill our fighting hole, and if we were in unfriendly territory, we would wind up sleeping in it all night. On this particular day, a marine patrol was crossing a bridge when the monsoon struck and two of the grunts were washed away. I saw four of the men from second squad half raise their hands to indicate that they would volunteer. Whitey stood to also volunteer and I found myself standing next to him. Whether this was a way to further gain acceptance into the unit or if it was a true gesture of brotherhood I still to this day am not sure. Maybe the fact that Sergeant Mason, who had been kind to me when I first arrived in-country, was leading the patrol had something to do with it.

When we arrived at the bridge we found several marines and some local villagers. The river was swollen past the banks but had calmed down since the rain ended. Sergeant Mason told us that they were making arrangements with the locals to rent one of their boats so we could go downstream to try to find our men. We lit our cigarettes and waited. A short while later we were floating down the middle of the river. I was a little shocked when I first saw our mode of transportation. Where did these villagers get an aluminum boat? I had seen sampans in the waterways but this was unlike anything I had seen ridden before by the South Vietnamese. The thought ran through my mind that this was probably a "Black Market Special." It had no motor so we were forced to paddle our way along. It was large enough to hold ten men, which, with the addition of the three marines we met at the bridge, equaled our number. The most worrisome characteristic to me was the fact that it virtually had no bulkheads. The sides flared out into wing like ends offering no cover.

After about a half-hour of traveling down the middle of the river we came around a bend. I started feeling uneasy as I noticed that there was thick jungle on both sides. I thought this would be a perfect place for an ambush. The enemy could fire on us from safe cover while we would be hopelessly exposed. I was starting to feel better about the situation as we paddled on uneventfully for some time, but just as we started to go under another bridge

I heard some rounds going over my head. We immediately turned outboard, half to the left and half to the right, and started firing. Since there was no cover in the boat we tried to lay down on the bottom. There was no room for all of us to assume a full prone position so we wound up on top of one another shooting wildly. We were so close together we were shooting our M16s right next to one another's heads. The ringing caused by the close firing was so loud that it caused a permanent partial hearing loss in my left ear.

Some of the men regained their senses, sat up in a crouch, and paddled like hell. They got us to a spot where it was impossible to get to us from either shore. No one was wounded. Once again I had been in a situation totally out of my control and survived. If there were no place to paddle to safety, we could have been caught in the open with the enemy firing into us until we were all dead. If the enemy had RPGs (Rocket Propelled Grenades) or mortars, they could have sunk us.

We never found the marines that day. Later Sergeant Mason told us some villagers found them down river. It only cost Uncle Sam two cartons of C-Rations to buy back their dead and bloated bodies.

The rest of the operation consisted of search and destroy missions, sweeps, ambushes and patrols, and a few more pitched battles. I was getting shot at, and I was firing back mostly with my head up. When the operation officially ended on July 31 I was still alive and in one piece. I didn't have to be told that the operation had been a success. The main indication of success for me was that the gun team was intact. After the operation they gave us an in-country R & R at China Beach. It was here that I first learned how much I had changed in so short a time.

When we first entered the area, we were told to store our weapons. We would not be allowed to carry our firearms within the limits of China Beach unless we were given specific assignments that would require us to do so. Although I was left with my K-Bar, I still felt extremely vulnerable. After being under fire for a prolonged period of time, I didn't realize how much a part of me my weapon had become. When Moon, Whitey, Johnson and I got off the six-by's that dropped us off at the main PX in China Beach, we were immediately surrounded by a score of small Vietnamese children. They were laughing and, holding their hands out, shouting, "G.I., G.I., you give me cigarette. G.I., you give me chocolate, you give me money." I was laughing myself as they completely encircled me until I felt a hand from behind reach into the lower leg pocket of my jungle utility trousers. Without thought or a moment's hesitation I immediately swung my arm back and heard a smack as my fist struck flesh. When I spun around I saw a child who looked to be about five years old on the ground bleeding from the mouth. He was unconscious as Moon stooped over him to check him out. When I felt a hand going into my pocket, the first thing I thought was that somebody was planting a bomb or explosive on me. Once I struck out I realized it was just a child trying to steal candy or money from me, things I would normally give freely. I was devastated. I've always loved children. To this day some of the greatest and most loving moments of my life have been spent with my children, grandchildren, nieces and nephews. To me, harming a child is the greatest of all sins. I waited breathlessly as Moon brought the Vietnamese boy around. He said the boy was not hurt badly and put a small dressing on his lip. I bent down and gave the boy some candy and some MPCs (Military Pay Certificates) that could be used as money. He grabbed my offerings and scurried away. Instead of pressing me for more loot, the other children dispersed and I was left standing there, feeling like an evil ogre.

This wasn't me, was it? I was finding it harder and harder to recognize myself. We continued walking toward the beach and no one mentioned the incident again.

During the day we were free to swim in the South China Sea, play volleyball on the beach and drink in the clubs. We enjoyed the hospitality of SeaBees (members of a Naval construction battalion) that were stationed near by. They graciously opened up their air-conditioned mess halls to us where we ate off of real dishes and had cold ice cream. They even invited us to a USO show that featured a rock band and some very pretty young girls from Australia.

Near the China Beach installation was located the main POW compound in the northern part of I Corps. While we were free to relax during the day they decided to put us to work at night. Our team was to man a machine gun tower when the sun went down. It was built of wood and corrugated tin. It was about twenty feet in the air with steps leading up into the center of the top. The roof was also made of wood and corrugated tin and the tower looked over the compound with an unrestricted field of fire. From one side of the tower was a view of Marble Mountain and from another you could almost make out Freedom Hill.

We first entered the tower a little before nighttime and I could clearly see the POWs below me. I knew as night came they would be restricted to their barracks and the flood lights in and around the camp would illuminate the scene. As I stared at these men I wondered if any of them had been involved in any of the battles of Allenbrook. I tried to think of what I would do if I found out that any of them had been involved in that first ambush I had participated in. I think I might have asked them if they were as afraid as I had been. There were other questions that I would like to have asked and one that I knew I could never ask. That question would have been about their families.

✬ ✬ ✬

I stayed with the 27th for about three more weeks and bonded with Moon, Whitey and Johnson in the short amount of time we spent together. After China Beach we continued to patrol our TAOR from our base camp in the "Riviera Area". The 27th had originally been formed as a support unit but Tet had changed that. They had achieved great success on the battlefield but had also suffered many casualties. The last combat action we shared together was an extremely memorable one.

The word came that the NVA overran a main bridge in our TAOR. We quickly marched to the sight. Our first charge caught them off guard and we pushed them off the bridge. We started to set up our defensive positions when they counter attacked and we were repelled from the bridge in turn. Reinforcements joined us and we once again successfully took the bridge. A heavy downpour of rain erupted and it became impossible for either side to continue the hostilities. We were ordered to dig in and prepare for another countercharge.

Our dead and wounded were rounded up and put in a safe place behind our side of the bridge. A platoon sergeant from 3rd Platoon Lima came over to our team and told us to set up our gun in a half destroyed bunker on the side of the bridge. I knew him to be a spit and polish Korean War veteran. He was known for his square-jawed countenance and the sawed-off shotgun he carried. He was also noted for going by the book. It wasn't good enough for him to have us just get in the bunker and use it for cover. He ordered us to rip the bunker apart and literally start rebuilding it from scratch.

The bunker was reinforced with ammunition boxes that had been placed in the sides of the dirt walls. Shelling by both us and the NVA had loosened the boxes from the sides and destroyed some of them. He told us to pull the boxes out and replace them with fresh ammo crates. The rain was falling unmercifully and the bunker was filling quickly with water. As I hurried to pull the damaged boxes out of the sides of the dirt walls, huge rats came scurrying out from behind them. We batted some of them out of the bunker but I knew a few of them remained.

We finished the renovation just as the water reached the top of the bunker and the NVA started to shell us. While I was waiting for the bombardment to end I froze as I saw the hairy back of one of the large rats dart across the top of the water. I gripped my rifle as my gaze skimmed the surface trying to get a fix on where the rodent had gone. I shouted to the team that we had company and I stayed up the rest of the night in abject terror.

When dawn came the enemy had withdrawn and so, it seemed, had our bunker mate. The order came to send the 27th Regiment back to the world. Moon and Whitey were going home. Johnson was transferred to the 5th and I was going to the 7th. I felt a profound sense of sadness and loss as I said good-bye to these good men. I never saw any of them again. I pray they all made it home safely.

Although I now felt somewhat more competent, I was still filled with uncertainty I knew I had to manage the fear that was always with me. It took constant willpower for me to overcome it in order to do my job and stay sane. I lost the luxury of planning for the distant future, the next week or even the next day. The entirety of my energy and concentration was now focused on staying alive in the current moment. For a short while I had brothers, comrades in arms to count on under fire to help keep me alive. Now, I was to go to the 7th Marines the same way I came to Vietnam and the 27th. It would be the same way I would leave, as well: alone.

Caption: "China Beach"

Top-In front of PX. L-R: Me, Sheeposh, Speakman, Thibadeaux. Bottom: Me, Gun Tower main POW compound Da Nang

Welcome to the "Nam"

3/27 Base Camp

CHAPTER TWO

DODGE CITY

South Vietnam
I Corps
September 14, 1968

They woke us up just before dawn. The word came to "Saddle-up!" and I quickly stirred to get my gear together. Being out in "Indian Country" I was used to moving fast in response to a given order. This wasn't like being at base camp. Out here the officers and noncoms didn't waste their breath on non-essential commands, nor did they screw with you for the sake of screwing with you. Out here it was life and death and everyone knew it. So when the word came to "Saddle-up" I did it as fast as I could.

I had been sleeping on my stomach and found the "John Wayne Can Opener" and the rosary my father had given me, which I wore around my neck, to be quite uncomfortable. I took both off in order to get some sleep. My father had sent the rosary to Rome to be blessed by the Pope when I first enlisted. I considered it a lucky charm and had not removed it since I had gotten in-country. That morning as I rushed to get squared away I forgot to put them back on.

As we formed up in our companies, platoons and squads, the word started to filter down that we were headed back to Dodge

City. Dodge City was appropriately named. It was about fourteen miles southwest of Da Nang and, like the American frontier town it was named after, one could always be assured of getting into a gunfight there. The NVA would try to launch attacks against Da Nang using Dodge City as a base. As a matter of fact we had just been out there two weeks before to drive back a contingent of NVA regulars. Unlike in other wars, however, when ground was captured and usually remained secure, in Vietnam there was a tendency to keep taking the same ground over and over again.

My skills as an Infantry M60 Machine Gunner had been well-honed when I was with the 27th so I was a little taken back by the situation I found when I got to the 7th. It seems the weapons squad leader had been promoted to weapons platoon leader and he was about to designate someone from the gun team to be the four-man team leader and as a result the team gunner. When I got to the 7th I immediately sized up the situation and realized that the person who was chosen to be leader and gunner had never been in combat, let alone fired an M60 in combat. I had seen enough fighting and death to be absolutely clear and certain of what I told the weapons platoon leader. I said that around base camp I would listen to my team leader but out in the bush, I would do what was necessary to stay alive. To my surprise, based on my confident demeanor, I was made team leader and hence chose myself as gunner. Out there it was life and death and everyone knew it.

I had been on some patrols and ambushes and some combat search and destroy missions with the 7th but nothing to match the intensity and fierceness of my days with the 27th. That morning, however, I felt that this was about to change.

We started out before the sun had fully risen. Before too long it was high in the sky. Someone mentioned that the temperature for that day was supposed to be about 103 degrees. The amount of gear carried by a "grunt" (Infantryman) is hard to imagine. As a gunner I carried my M60 with a hundred-round belt of 7.62 ammunition on a jungle sling that crossed my chest for easy access and weighed about thirty pounds. In addition I carried a rucksack holding three to four days worth of C-Rations, a web belt to which was attached my .45 caliber pistol, several magazines of ammunition, as many canteens of water as I could get, which was usually four, and five to six hand grenades. These items weighed in at from fifty to sixty pounds. On top of this we were advised to wear our flak jackets. Since flak jackets usually could not stop a direct hit by an AK-47 round grunts in the bush usually doffed the jackets if the heat was too oppressive.

There were two companies on this march, Lima (L Company), which was my company, as well as Mike (M Company). By the book a company consisted of four platoons. Each platoon had four squads. A squad was supposed to have fifteen men each. Therefore four squads of fifteen men each equaled sixty men in a platoon. A company consisted of four platoons so theoretically there were 240 men in a company. Attached to a company were at least two four-man weapons teams each consisting of an M60 gunner and two or three ammo bearers depending on how the gun team leader organized his team. He could either appoint a gunner or he could choose to be the gunner himself. Added to these were the squad leaders, company commanders, radio men and mortar support. Unfortunately during those days in Vietnam the tactical strength of the units was never where it should be. There were times when there were only seven men in a squad—and sometimes fewer than that—so it was hard to know exactly how many troops you actually had at any given time. It was not unheard of for new replacements to get killed as soon as they entered into battle. And so, with two companies that should have numbered over 480 men, we were probably on our way with about 350.

When we reached the outskirts of Dodge City we fell into our units to await our orders. I was still feeling a little uneasy. I had been with these men before but I had an overwhelming feeling this was going to be big. Never before had I been on such a large- sized operation with them and we certainly had come loaded for bear. I didn't know these men well enough to know how much I could trust them in a large firefight. I hadn't had enough time to feel how they would react. I had to rely on the reputation of the 7th and the fact that they were marines and to concentrate on doing my job.

When the squad leaders came to brief us I could sense the gravity in their demeanor. As they unveiled the plan I could tell someone had told them that this was going to be one hell of a fight. The strategy was that Lima Company was to proceed ahead and set up a blocking force. This was to be a perpendicular line stretched out as far as it could go with four feet between each man. Mike Company was then to move on line through a designated area where an NVA Battalion had been spotted, sweep them between us, hammer on anvil, and annihilate them.

As we moved to our position all kinds of thoughts went through my mind. As I mentioned before I had been on larger operations with the 27th but this had the feel of something different.

As a young child I would set up my toy soldiers in the living room in full battle lines and stare at them for hours. I would not move anything physically but would act out the charges and countercharges in my head, taking note of the casualties from both sides and the ground given and lost. Sometimes I would sense that I had set up my troops incorrectly and would play it out to the end with my side falling back. This, for some reason, had that same feeling.

By the time we got to our designated area the searing rays of the sun were beating down on us and the tropical heat was merciless. A lot of us were trying to quench our thirst with the hot water from our plastic canteens. There was a tree line about one hundred meters directly to the right of our line. Our company commander ordered two marines to go forward and recon the tree line. As soon as the two marines were halfway out they were cut down by automatic fire. At the same time we started to receive incoming fire from the tree line and from the tall elephant grass that was all around us. We were surrounded. When the fire starting coming in at us, we could hear the crackle of distant gunfire to our rear. There was no doubt in my mind that the same thing that was happening to us was also happening to Mike Company. The enemy had been waiting for us and now they had us pinned down.

After the initial bursts of incoming fire hit us we were given orders to reform from the blocking position to a circular defensive position. Since I was one of two gun teams assigned to Lima my orders were to set up and face the tree line from which most of the fire was coming. While the grunts got into position I sprayed the tree line with steady controlled bursts the same way I had seen done in countless war movies. Somehow that thought calmed me as I tried to detach myself from the situation. This worked until I realized they were shooting at me. Then all I could think of was that in gun school the instructor told us that the life expectancy of an infantry machine gunner in combat was about seven seconds. The objective in a firefight is to gain fire superiority, and the best way to do that is to silence the enemy's automatic weapons.

The orders were coming in fast and furious now. The grunts were ordered to charge the tree line and try to displace the enemy. The first assault failed and the marines were driven back. It was my job to lay cover fire for them on their assault and spray the trees in case there were any snipers in them. After our first assault they countercharged and came at us. They didn't get very far before we put a withering barrage of small arms and automatic fire into them. After they pulled back they set into positions from which they could fire into our perimeter.

Since there was no urgent need to our front, some lieutenant came and tapped me on the shoulder and motioned for me and my team to follow him. It seemed that the other gun team had managed to cook off a round in the chamber, disabling the gun. This would happen to an M60 machine gun if it was fired too much without giving it a chance to cool down. Most of us carried some kind of lubricant to try to keep the barrel cool because although the book said that you would be issued a spare barrel, it very rarely happened. The second gun team had been positioned off to the right to stop an enemy charge on that flank. The gun had gone down along with two casualties and the enemy was slowly gaining ground behind the tall elephant grass. I found a spot to set up my gun and then I waited. All of a sudden I heard whizzes and snapping all around me. The enemy was starting another assault by firing into our position. They knew that the original gun on that flank was down but we were hoping they didn't realize another gun had been brought up to replace it.

As the rounds whirled through the tall grass I sat there totally helpless and filled with fear. I was sure John Wayne or Gary Cooper or Errol Flynn never felt such fear. My fight-or-flight mechanism was totally out of whack. I couldn't open up yet because we were waiting for them to get closer and into view. I couldn't run because there was no where to run *to*. Not being able to do either gave me an enormous headache. It also amplified the sounds of the rounds buzzing past me. There were several times when I could even feel the breeze of them going past my head.

Just when I thought I could stand it no longer they came into view, crouching at first, then standing up and rushing straight at us. By this time we had accumulated two squads from the line. Upon command we all opened up, and the ensuing staccato of gunfire was deafening. When the order came to cease fire there was not a single enemy left standing. This was the first time I actually saw men I shot at go down. While it was happening I felt that I was in a state of suspended animation. Everything seemed sharp and extremely focused. Nothing before or since has ever been as clear as the sight of those men falling, their bodies writhing in unnatural spasms while their life's blood sprayed from the bullet holes I put in their bodies. What troubled me even more was that I was able to go on seemingly unaffected. Not until years later would I pay the psychic price of that encounter.

I was ordered back to the front of the line. We were going to try one last assault. This was to give us a chance to get our wounded out of the middle of the battlefield. We could hear them screaming for help. The NVA had a habit of deliberately wounding a man so that when he cried for help they could kill him and anyone else who would come to save him. The plan was that the grunts would throw out Willy Peter (White phosphorous) smoke grenades. Once the smoke had been released I was to open up and walk my gun along the front of the opposing tree line. I had set up my gun on a small knoll with a good view of the battlefield, as I didn't want to hit any of my men as they rushed out to save the wounded.

The smoke went out and as I started firing, the ground suddenly exploded into bits of dirt that sprayed all over me. My assistant gunner had just gone to his knees to start to coat my barrel with LSA oil when a round caught him full in the side of his face. This was the marine I replaced as team leader and gunner upon entering the 7th. Just as I realized that his blood and parts of his face were covering me, I felt a sharp pain in my left arm. It was like a red-hot poker had been jammed into my left forearm.

Even though I had been taught not to look at a wound in order to avoid shock, I did look down quickly and saw blood gushing straight out as if it were a fountain.

Somehow I had the presence of mind to slide down the small side of the knoll. The pain was unbearable. I was actually angry that it hurt this badly. In the movies when the hero was hit in the arm, he merely wrapped a bandage around it and pushed on. There definitely was more going on here. Someone called for a corpsman, then it seemed like a very long time before one got to me. He shot me with morphine and the pain started to slip away. I started to shout at him, asking him why it had hurt that much. After a look at the wound he started laughing and said I had extensive nerve damage. As a matter of fact he could see exposed nerves in my arm.

It was about this time that our strategy changed. Previously our company commander had been reluctant to call in air strikes or artillery. He felt we were too close to the enemy and the lines were too fluid to avoid dropping rounds on friendly troops. By this time however, it was clear we were at a stalemate. As I lay at the bottom of the knoll being administered to by the corpsman my mind was trying to get a handle on the situation. Under the growing influence of the morphine, the dull pain in my arm and the constant gunfire, the scene started to take on a surreal atmosphere. They were bringing other wounded marines to my area. We were told to hold on. Helicopters were coming to get us but were delayed because of the impending air strikes. Suddenly the ground under me shook as Navy pilots dropped 500 pound bombs into the tree line and around our position. About forty-five minutes later there was silence. It seemed the enemy had been suppressed.

Immediately after the air strikes subsided we heard the whirring of the rotors on the evacuation helicopters. I received a second shot of morphine while waiting to be "dusted off." I barely remember being helped on to one of the choppers. My memory is vivid of one young marine on board who had his hands on his stomach holding on to his exposed intestines.

We got back to a field medical unit. There were dozens of marines in all stages of injury. Corpsmen and nurses were going over the wounded determining who were the neediest and whom should be taken care of first. The back of my arm had been blown out, exposing nerves. I had bled so badly that the left side of my body was totally covered with blood. When a corpsman took a quick look at me I heard him say, "Amputation!" At that moment my entire world came off its axis. I had contemplated dying in this war. I had also thought of being wounded, wearing my " Red Badge of Courage" as a testament to bearing the brunt of battle and going through my right of passage, but an amputation? My ego would not process this. I rejected it with every molecule of my body. I yelled a loud, long expletive. Then the first miracle of my life occurred. A navy doctor had been passing me on his way to the OR. He stopped to take a look at me and asked the corpsman who had pronounced my sentence what was going on. When the corpsman repeated his diagnosis of amputation the doctor said he thought he could save the arm.

They rushed me into surgery. They were in such a hurry that I could still feel the cold scissors as the doctor began to cut through my arm. I let out a loud groan and they administered more anesthesia. The next thing I remember is waking up in a bed at the naval hospital in Da Nang. There was a throbbing pain in my arm. It was heavily wrapped in gauze but it was still attached. They had saved it! There was something else I noticed as I started coming to. Around my neck was a tag. It looked like a baggage tag from a commercial airliner. On this tag, however, were only five letters:"CONUS." This stood for "Continental United States." This was the winning lottery ticket, the gold wrapper from the Wonka Bar, the all-access pass for a Beatles concert.

I was going home. I was leaving this hell on earth where death and dismemberment were constant companions. I couldn't think much about making plans for when I got home. I knew it would be a long road of hospitals, operations and rehab. I was just nineteen years old but already felt like a forty-year-old man. It wasn't until 1994 that I read in the "Declassification of Combat After Action Reports" that I found out we had run into seventy-two fortified enemy bunkers. Our adversaries had been the D-3

Sapper Battalion of the 36th Regiment of the NVA. The fight had continued through the night and into the next day after I had been evacuated. We suffered 120 casualties ,but all I knew was that I was going home.

I wondered how I would be received. There had been disturbing stories of how some were treated when getting back to the world but I felt they had been exaggerated. It would all be Disneyland after this.

CHAPTER THREE

"In the Kingdom of the Blind, the One-Eyed Man is King"

Yokosuka Japan
Naval Hospital
20 September, 1968

I traveled to the naval hospital in Yokosuka, Japan on a stretcher in a converted C-130. The huge transport plane had been gutted and stretchers had been affixed to the interior bulkheads. IV stands, monitors and other medical equipment were available for the wounded men. Air force nurses were there to administer medical attention as needed. The pain in my arm was still throbbing after the operations I received first in the field medical hospital and then at the main hospital facility in Da Nang.

The diagnosis had become clear. The ulna, radial and median nerves in my arm had been severed. My wrist bone had been shattered and the main forearm bone had been split in two. The AK-47 round had entered the front of my arm and bounced around inside my arm as the round was designed to do. It then blew a four-inch by three-inch section out of the backside of my arm. I was told that while I was in Japan I would be going through several operations to try to repair some of the damage and stabilize my condition. This would include putting pins in my arm, a plate in my wrist and then returning to the United States.

There I would be receiving further operations primarily for nerve repair and then therapy. The doctors had no idea how long this might take.

I listened to all this in a state of disbelief. I knew it was important to pay attention because my future was going to be affected but I couldn't connect the words to my reality. I had enlisted in the marines at the age of eighteen I was an unorganized, undisciplined, wild and self-absorbed teenager. The Marines tore me down and rebuilt me. They put me in the greatest physical shape of my life, gave me clarity of purpose and taught me that there was a greater good than my own self-interest. Through the rigors of Marine Corps boot camp I learned teamwork, perseverance, strength of character and the belief in being able to overcome great obstacles. The marines made me feel invincible. At the age of nineteen I went to war. Even as I saw death and dismemberment all around me I still believed I was bulletproof. In my mind I was the perfect male specimen. All women would want me and all men would want to be me. Now, naval doctors in starched white uniforms were telling me the best I could hope for was a withered arm with limited use.

The lessons taught to me by the Marine Corps would help me deal with these issues but at the time I was devastated. I sunk into a deep depression and talked to no one except to answer the questions of the doctors and nurses. I began to sink lower in my depression. During those days Naval Corpsmen were able to dispense drugs by doctors' orders. Some of the orders read, "As needed." Many of the corpsmen who were at the hospital had seen duty in Vietnam with combat marine units. If there was anyone combat marines looked up to and even revered it was the navy corpsman.

These "Angels on the Battlefield" were some of the most heroic men I have ever seen. In the midst of gun fire and explosions they would rush from marine to marine administering aid and comfort at great peril to their own lives. More than a few of them received the Medal of Honor and they saved many of our lives. By being attached to us, living as we did and witnessing our suffering and agonies, they developed a strong bonding and respect for the grunts under their care. As a result they truly became our brothers. Under these conditions when assigned to hospitals and care facilities for marines, they continued their desire to administer to our afflictions. When the orders were to administer pain killing drugs "As needed," their main concern was to alleviate the sufferings of their brothers whose bodies were recently mutilated. To some of us, "As needed" came to mean as needed to alleviate physical or *mental* pain, which at times could be almost as bad. I was starting to ask for drugs more often to stop my mental pain than my physical pain when the second miracle of my life occurred.

One day in early October a young marine was brought to the rack next to mine. I didn't think much about it then. He was just another grunt in from the meat grinder. His eyes were closed and his blanket was pulled up to his chin so I took a cursory look and went back to sleep. The next day as I was waking I heard some movement to my right. I turned in time to see several corpsmen, a doctor and a nurse at the rack of my new neighbor. With the blanket pulled down I saw the wounds that had been hidden the night before by the blanket. I immediately turned from the scene as my eyes filled with tears and I shuddered in an attempt to stop from crying out loud. The marine next to me was what we crudely referred to as a basket case: a quadruple amputee. The gauze around the stumps that the medical group was attempting to change were wet and stained with bright blood. When I had looked quickly at his face, his eyes were closed and he seemed to be sleeping. I couldn't bring my self to even try to think of what his thoughts would be when he came to the realization of his condition.

As I tried to calm down a new wave of soul-wrenching sadness washed over me. This time it was an eruption of guilt and shame. It started with the thought that here I was, depressed and despondent about what amounted to a minor injury compared to this poor soul next to me. The guilt that had been stirring inside me now was coming to the surface. The guilt I felt that I was alive while many others were not was almost too much to bear. The guilt of leaving my brothers behind in danger while I was safe in Japan was tormenting. The shame of feeling sorry for myself while those around me were far more seriously injured than I filled me with self-loathing. I cried inwardly for God to help me and soon fell back asleep.

The next morning as I awoke I felt a quiet calm throughout my body. Somehow my outlook on my situation started to change. My heart was lighter and I began to think of myself as being blessed. In my mind God had placed that young marine next to me to show me He was still looking out for me, just as he had placed that naval doctor next to me when I laid in triage ready to have my arm amputated that day in Dodge City. I suddenly realized that God was always placing miracles in our lives but it was up to us to recognize and accept them. I believed there was also a miracle waiting for that marine lying next to me and even though I could not imagine what it might be, I prayed he would recognize it when it happened. As my thoughts lifted, my actions soon followed. I started to ask for pain medication only to alleviate my physical pain. To this day, after all my recent surgeries and painful procedures, I am hard-pressed to ask for or take pain medication unless it becomes absolutely necessary. Given the serious and recent wounds in our ward I looked for ways to alleviate the depression there. I had a tendency towards gallows humor as evidenced by one of my favorite pranks.

When someone was to go to surgery his name, procedure and after-care were all written on a blackboard so the incoming staff would know what was to happen that day. The blackboard was in the ward so the patient was also aware of the schedule and could prepare himself for the upcoming operation. A couple of times after a marine would come back from some serious surgery I would re-enter his name on the board while he was asleep. I would be woken up by a loud expletive as my poor target awakened, bleary-eyed, only to see his name on the board scheduled for another operation. My co-conspirators and I would laugh hysterically and then rush over to the poor guy to assure him that it was just a hoax. I'm sure that if they could, the patients would have instantly risen and caused us great bodily injury, but it usually turned out that our laughter and good nature would bring a smile and sense of relief to our victims.

Stunts like these had a tendency to lift the mood and almost made us feel like irresponsible teenagers again, if just for a little while. It was also comical to watch the influx of patients to the wards every weekend. It seemed that the sailors and marines who were stationed in Yokosuka did not take kindly to the transient troops who came to the bars looking for female companionship. The local girls were already spoken for and the battles for a change of their affection would cause numerous men to be rushed to the hospital.

As time went by I became more ambulatory between my operations. With my new outlook on life I became the goodwill ambassador of the ward. I'd go from rack to rack and talk to my fellow patients. Some were eager to talk, some would speak curtly and a few would not respond at all. After going through what I had gone through I recognized that those young warriors were on an emotional roller-coaster. They were mentally going through the various stages of their condition as I had done: denial; happiness for being alive; guilt for feeling happiness when their dead brothers had been left behind; and bouts of self-pity, quickly followed by feelings of shame for having those thoughts. Under it all was a blurred vision of an uncertain future. I was sure these feelings were universal in all wounded soldiers from every war ever fought.

Back then most of us smoked. Those who had a desire to would walk or were wheeled to the day room for snacks, sodas, cigarettes, companionship and conversation. We talked about a lot of things. We talked about what units we were with, where we had served and where we were wounded. We talked about home, our families and women. We talked a lot about women. We knew that our contemporaries who chose not to serve were reaping the benefits of a new and changing world. We were reading about the sexual revolution going on back in the world. We were sent Playboy magazines that showed women in a whole new way and we couldn't wait to immerse ourselves in this liberated culture of bra-burning and free love. We talked of all these things but just barely spoke of the deeper issues. It was too soon, the scars too deep, to bring to the surface. We weren't ready to share our personal experiences of the war, if our girlfriends back home had been faithful or if we had changed so much they wouldn't love us anymore. We didn't talk about how we would live back in the world with our wounds and disfigurements. It was enough at that time to share a safe haven from the war with brothers-in-arms with similar experiences.

Some of the things we were reading in the newspapers sent to us from the world were disturbing. There were thousands of people protesting on the streets of the United States against the war. There were politicians proclaiming we couldn't win in Vietnam and should pull out immediately. This was a puzzlement, as most of us were veterans of the bloody battles of Tet and the offensive of the summer of '68. The North Vietnamese communists had launched all out attacks in order to defeat us as they had done to the French at the Battle of Dien Bien Phu. On January 31, 1968 they launched attacks over the entire country of South Vietnam. Every major city, village and provincial capital was hit. Battles raged in Saigon, Da Nang, Hue City, Khe Sahn, Lang Vei and dozens more. In Hue City the marines fought fierce battles in house-to-house fighting. At Khe Sahn six thousand marines were surrounded by forty thousand North Vietnamese soldiers in a siege that was ultimately broken. The North Vietnamese were totally beaten and they conquered nothing. The Viet Cong, their guerilla cadres, were decimated. They ceased to be an effective fighting force in the south and after Tet most operations were run by the NVA. Their casualties were astronomical.

In the summer of 1968 they attempted another major offensive primarily in I Corps and were once again thoroughly defeated. We thought it ironic that we, who defeated, killed and wounded tens of thousands of the enemy and saved the cities of South Vietnam from their communist invaders were being told by the politicians who would not allow total victory that we couldn't win the war. It was their rule that we couldn't invade North Vietnam in order to bring the war to an end. It was their rule that we couldn't go after the enemy if they ran away across the border to Cambodia. It was their rule that we couldn't destroy the Ho Chi Minh Trail that brought ammunition, weapons and supplies to the NVA fighting in the south.

When we read of what was happening to our brothers when they returned to the world we became angry and frustrated. How dare they treat us this way? Who were they to judge us? Most of us were volunteers. We weren't victims. We enlisted out of a sense of duty, patriotism and love of our country no matter what our backgrounds were. We had listened to John Kennedy when he said, "Ask not what your country can do for you. Ask what you can do for your country." We read about some of our brothers actually joining the protesters to condemn our actions. We wouldn't find out until we got home how hard it was to resist the anti-war movement. We were young and wanted to fit in. The call of the anti-war nihilists was seductive. They seemed to be saying, " Join us, rebuke what you did, show the world that we are right and we'll let you into our world of sex, drugs and rock 'n' roll. Join us and condemn the war and those who fought it and we will honor you. Reject us and we will include you in the ranks of murders and baby-killers." Later we would find out that one of the founders of the "Vietnam Veterans Against the War" was a liar who had never been to Vietnam. We would also find out that before he was a senator, John Kerry sat before members of the United States Congress and spouted unsubstantiated horror stories about what we did to Vietnamese citizens.

We learned that during a battle in the A Shau Valley Senator Ted Kennedy said the heroic 101st Airborne weren't good enough and would never be able to take "Hamburger Hill." Of course, after days of bloody fighting, the 101st took "Hamburger Hill." To this day I don't recall having heard Senator Kennedy's apologies. It must be nice to be able to criticize those who are risking their lives to keep you free and safe so you can reap more than your share of all the benefits this country has to offer.

Not knowing what was ahead of us, we tried to push those feelings of anger and frustration down deep inside of us. We knew what we did and we knew why we did it. We'd let them know when we got back to the world.

✡ ✡ ✡

I was to have one more operation before being sent back home. I knew my fighting days were over but what was next? Where would I be sent? There was talk that you would not necessarily be sent to a hospital near your home or even in your state. We heard it would come down to what type of injury you had and the capacity of the hospital. I knew the closest naval hospital to my home on the south side of Chicago was the Great Lakes Naval Hospital in Glenview, Illinois. I went to sleep every night praying I would be sent there.

My last surgery in Japan was finally scheduled. They would be cutting a little bit more of the exit wound on the backside of my arm for easier access. They would apply a long arm cast from the knuckles of my hand to just below my left shoulder. They would leave a cut out in the back to allow the exit wound to continue to heal. The cast was to remain on my arm for the next year and a half. Then I found out the great news: I would indeed be going to the Great Lakes Naval Hospital. They had a good orthopedic wing and they had room for me. Later on Great Lakes would be so filled with our wounded I would be transferred to the Lakeside Veterans' Administration Hospital on Huron Street in downtown Chicago while I was still in the marines. A marine liaison was established and we were placed with veterans of former wars.

I woke from my operation with some discomfort and found the heavy plaster cast on my arm in a sling. As I was coming to, my eyes were drawn to the blackboard. I broke out in a broad smile as I recognized my name on the schedule as one who was set for another surgery the next day. Upon seeing my reaction, a group of my fellow patients came to my rack laughing and asking how I was.

In a few days I was ready to go back to the world, the land of the "Big PX," the land of home and family. Once again I tried not to think of anything beyond that vision. Once again I was to leave my new friends, never expecting to see them again. I was leaving as I had arrived, alone. I called my family a few days after arriving in Yokosuka and assured them I was okay. It was a good thing I called because I found out the first Western Union Telegraph they received had limited information. It stated that I was wounded but they didn't know exactly how I was wounded, how grave the wound was or where I was at the time. My family had tracked me down through the Red Cross. They knew I was in Japan but not the extent of my wounds. I assured them I was okay and for them not to worry. When I called, my mother answered the phone. When she heard my voice she immediately handed the phone to my sister. I could hear her crying in the background as I explained my situation to my sister and relayed the itinerary for my care. I called back once the schedule for my return had been solidified.

The day finally arrived when they put me in another converted C-130 on a stretcher. A huge chapter of my life was ending. I had been trained as a combat marine. I fought a war. I killed men, was almost killed myself and I was injured for life. I saw friends die and young men maimed. My heart and soul had been scarred and I wondered if I would ever be able to recover what I had lost. I had been to Hawaii, Okinawa, Vietnam and Japan. I swam in the South China Sea. I experienced all this and I was still just nineteen years old. A new chapter of my life was about to begin. It would start at the same place it had all begun, with my family.

CHAPTER FOUR

The Beginning

Chicago Illinois
1890s to 1960s

Both my maternal and fraternal grandparents came from Italy. My maternal grandparents came from Sicily and my fraternal grandfather came from Terra Nova, his future wife from Calabria. They came in the late 1800s for the same reasons that tens of thousands of others were making the trek across the ocean: the promise of a new life in a land where it didn't matter what your father did for a living. A land where you could rise above your station of birth and be whatever you wanted to be and attain whatever it was that you were willing to work for and sacrifice for. A place to raise your children and give them a step up on the ladder of the American Dream.

Salvatore Felicicchia and Prudence Badali, my mother's parents, did have an interesting story. When they were in Sicily, Salvatore was a foreman for an olive grove where Prudence was a field hand. As the story goes, Salvatore fell in love with Prudence but his family would not stand for their relationship. Although an overseer in an olive grove was not the top of the social strata in Sicily, it surely was above that of a lowly olive picker. When Salvatore was told that he would be disowned if he pursued Prudence he decided to take the lovely Prudence and migrate to America.

Some of Prudence's family lived in Canada and some lived in Chicago. After a short visit to each location they finally decided to settle on the south side of Chicago on Kensington and Indiana in the Roseland Community. There my grandfather borrowed some money, bought some land and opened a grocery store with an apartment in the rear and two coldwater flats upstairs. This was the first house I remember.

Salvatore and Prudence, who I sadly don't remember, had eight children that lived, three boys and five girls. By the time I was five we were living above the store, which was being operated by my aunt Josephine and her husband Bill. They lived in the back of the store with their daughter Barbara, and above them and directly across from us were my aunt Grace, her husband Brownie and their five kids: Joanne, Tony, Prudence, Bruno and Mary Ann.

Our cold-water flat had a front room, a small kitchen and two bedrooms. In these cramped quarters were my mother, Rose, my father (also named Sal), me and my three sisters: Josephine, Prudence and Kathleen. Since there were only two bedrooms I shared one with my sisters. I slept in one bed and the three of them slept in another. My sisters were to become heroes to me in later life but back then they were just annoying. Even though I was the youngest and only boy and they treated me well, I still acted out as a spoiled brat.

There were ten cousins growing up in basically the same house. How much fun was that! I'll get back to this after we find out what Pasquale and Josephine did when they got to America.

It is said that Pasquale Lufrano (the "u" was closed at Ellis Island in a clerical error) was a shoemaker in Terra Nova who also blocked hats. There is a family legend that the famous Florshiem once asked Pasquale to go into business with him but that story has never been verified. Josephine Vinezeano, the future wife of Pasquale, had come to America at the age of three. If you've ever seen the women from Calabria you were likely enthralled with their beauty. They are noted for their dark, smooth skin, which keeps them ageless, and their tiny chiseled facial features that look finely-drawn.

Not finding any shoemaking business that would make him enough money to start a family, Pasquale went to work laying track out west after he arrived in the country. When the track was completed and he was let go he moved to the west side of Chicago in the neighborhood where the University of Illinois at Chicago Circle campus now stands. At that time there was a growing Italian community centered around the Jane Adams Hull House which offered help and refuge to the Italian community. The area was also dedicated to Mother Cabrini who later became the first American saint.

When Josephine Vinezeano met Pasquale Lofrano at the age of 15 it was love at first sight.

After a brief courtship they were married and immediately started on their family. In the end they had ten children, seven boys and three girls. Even though there are only three left from both sides of the family, I feel the same nostalgic happiness and warmth for those that are gone as I do for those who are here. It was my good fortune that both families eventually wound up in the same place and I was the recipient of so much love and extended family interaction.

How did Pasquale and Josephine Lofrano finally move to Kensington Avenue from the west side? The story goes like this: My grandfather started a small shoeshine and shoe repair shop where he also blocked hats. His shop was in front of a saloon where my father and uncle Nick tended bar. My grandfather was still having a little trouble with the language so he didn't understand who a major patron of the saloon was. In fact that major patron was an infamous gangster. He was a hit man for the old "42" gang, a precursor of the Capone mob. The hoodlums that would come and go past the shoeshine stand and into the saloon were deferential to my grandfather, father and uncle. They liked the hard-working immigrant and his sons. He reminded them of their fathers and they treated him with respect.

One particular afternoon the son of a mob boss was shot outside the saloon. A man ran in and put a gun in one of the drawers behind the bar. A policeman entered soon after and asked my uncle if he had seen anything.

Although my uncle had recognized the man with the gun he said nothing. This seemed to please the policeman who smiled knowingly and walked out without searching the bar.

From that time on my father and his brothers were constantly being recruited by the gang. It's said that my grandmother put her foot down and told Pasquale they were going to have to move far away. As fate would have it they moved no more than a half block from my mother's family.

This is about as close as my family got to the Italian mob. My mother's family had to move after their store was blown up by the "Black Hand" for not paying tribute to the local boss. After a short stay in Oregon they worked it out with their parish priest who happened to be a relative of the local boss.

After the Lofranos were settled in their new house my father became friends with my mother's brothers, Augostino (called "Stiddy") and Joe. It didn't take him long to notice their sister Rose and they say that every afternoon he used to sit in the window of "The Italian Young Man's Pleasure Club" and watch for her to come home from work.

Rose and Sal were married at Saint Anthony Church on Kensington and Prairie on June 8, 1940. By that time my mother's father was a big man in the neighborhood, running a successful store catering to the needs of the burgeoning Italian community. My mother wore a white satin dress and the couple had a three-layer cake with a decorative top out from which flew white doves.

My earliest recollections start at about the age of four or five. As I mentioned, I lived in a cold water flat, which means there was no hot water, no hot shower. When I was very young my mother would heat water in a large wash bucket and bathe me in it. As I got older we would go to Grandpa Lofrano's house and use his shower every Saturday night whether we needed it or not.

Before my grandfather and grandmother Felicicchia died they willed much of their land to Saint Anthony's Church, as their son Anthony had entered the Scalibrini Order. By the time I was in kindergarten my whole world was bound by our four flat, the school, the school playground and the rectory. Basically all I had to do was go down a flight of stairs and walk twenty-five feet to school. Was it any wonder I was always late?

Back then, the far south side of Chicago was like a patchwork quilt of ethnic inhabitants separated by religion, church and country of origin. The Italians lived, worshipped and went to school at Saint Anthony of Padua. There were Holy Rosary Irish, Holy Rosary Slovak, Saint Salomea a (Polish), Saint Louis of France and Saint Willibrord (Dutch).

We, of course, went to Saint Anthony. The best and worst thing about going to Saint Anthony's grammar school was the number of cousins who attended. Remember those ten first cousins that virtually lived in one place? Well, that doesn't count the other cousins from both sides who also attended the school. We were all ages from kindergarten to eighth grade. Odds were we would be in some of the same classes. This gave us an endless sense of family and terrific playmates during recess. The bad thing was that there were no secrets.

Once while in first grade I was caught carving up my wooden school desk with the end of a pencil that was missing the eraser from its metal holder. Sister Mary Jane took me to each of the school rooms and grades to display me as the criminal of the century who was shamed in the sight of God. I got a lot of guffaws from my cousins as well as a few discreet thumbs up until we got to my sister Prudy's room. She proceeded to tell the nun she didn't appreciate the inquisition I was going through. The nun promptly gave Prudy a detention and sent me home with a letter to my parents who continued the punishment on a different part of my body.

Another bad thing about going to the same school as your siblings and cousins is you are constantly being compared with those that had gone before you. Unfortunately for me, my sisters were not only brilliant but also well-behaved and helpful to the nuns. "Why can't you be like your sisters" became my middle name.

During that time in the neighborhood the men either worked at the Sherwin Williams paint factory or the Pullman Shops. My father worked at Sherwin Williams. It was a good job for those with only a high school education but the benefits were not great. My father had wanted to go to college but it was the

Depression, so due to the size of his family and his position in it was forced to go to work to help support his family. He remained a highly intelligent self-educated man whose opinions and ideas were sought after until the day he became too sick to respond.

The age of ten was a watershed year for me. It was the year when my parents finally bought a house, located on East 117th Street, and it was the year that my father started to get sick.

In those days we still had a doctor who made house calls, but although he was kind and committed his knowledge of complicated diseases was limited. Even though it took eighteen years from that point for the illness to finally take my father, what I remember is that my father went from a cane to crutches to a wheelchair in what seemed like rapid time. By the time we got him to the Chicago Rehabilitation Center for a diagnosis he was rapidly deteriorating and could hardly speak.

After a series of tests the doctors called us into the conference room. It was decided that since I was the male I would be the one to tell my father he had Amyotrophic Lateral Sclerosis, (ALS), otherwise known as Lou Gherig's Disease. I remember my father smiling and barely whispering, "I don't have cancer?" For his generation the "C" word was the sentence of death. He thought that if it wasn't cancer, everything would be okay. He had no idea of the horrors of ALS. He didn't realize that his muscles would deteriorate into nothing while his mind would stay sharp taking note of everything that was happening to him. He didn't realize in the end he wouldn't be able to chew his food and he would have to be fed through a tube going directly into his stomach.

In the time before he got sick up to and including his confinement to a wheelchair our house was constantly filled with relatives and friends. They would come for my mother's great food and desserts. Her coffee was famous for its taste and aroma, which she attributed to egg shells in the grinds and the old battered pot it was brewed in. The guests did not stop when my father became wheelchair bound. If anything the visits increased.

Before his sickness was diagnosed at Chicago Rehab he became weaker and weaker, but my uncles would come over and try to get him up and help him walk. I remember him straining to try to do the impossible not realizing that it would never work. His spirits were never dampened and I think that was one of the reasons people came around. To be around him was a blessing. To know he suffered without complaint gave people a sense of calm in his presence. He was an avid reader before his eyes went and when they did he would ask to be read to. He was a student of history and world events and could not only hold his own in discussions but he could make you see his point of view in a non-threatening way.

I think the best way to describe him is by the time our parish pastor finally came to see him. They had been good friends for many years and everyone wondered why Father Nalin had not come to visit my father sooner. They had not only been personal friends but my father had been very active in the church by being a member and president of the Holy Name Society, coaching youth baseball and raising funds for the new church. After a lengthy and pleasant visit filled with laughter and the telling of old stories my mother and I walked the priest to the front door. When we reached the vestibule Father Nalin grabbed my mother's arm and, with tears in his eyes, said, "Rose, I'm so ashamed. I found it hard to come to see Sal because I felt so sorry and despondent that such a good man was stricken with such a disease. I finally convinced myself to come to see him to cheer him up. Instead, he has lifted my spirits with his faith and good will. I am humbled by him." That's the effect my father had on people. They would come to cheer him up and he would actually lift them up. He was the kind of person that made you feel good just by being in his presence.

To give you an idea of how I was handling my father's deteriorating sickness at that time is to tell you it is said my mother never swore until I was born. As I mentioned, my three older sisters were not only smart but were also well mannered and when it came to helping my mother with the house while she was busy taking care of my father they were like angels from heaven.

In those days the family unit was definitely chauvinistic and in an Italian family with one boy it could be downright tyrannical. It was believed the natural order of things was that the daughters would grow up, get married, have children and become part of another man's house. The son would carry on the name and by doing so give the father a sort of immortality. Even though the daughters were greatly loved and cared for, it was to the sons that most attention and resources were given. My father was only half joking when he used to say that he was the king, I was the prince and my mother and sisters were the servers. This sounds pretty harsh today but, unfortunately, it wasn't far from the truth then.

For example, every Saturday morning the names of all the rooms in our house were put in a hat and each of my sisters reached into the hat and picked a slip of paper. On that slip were written two rooms, one hard room and one easier room to clean. They couldn't go out, talk to friends or watch TV until all rooms were done. They would put albums by Johnny Mathis and Frank Sinatra and Broadway hits like *My Fair Lady*, *West Side Story*, and *Camelot* on the Hi-Fi. On one of the slips of paper was written "The Monster's Room." This, of course, indicated my bedroom. I had finally gotten my own room. Even though it was as small as a closet and had no door, it was still mine. My sisters still slept in the same bedroom but that room was bigger and only two had to sleep in the same bed while the other had a bed to herself. While my bedroom was mine the responsibility to keep it clean was my sisters'. When they would complain, my father would tell them that boys shouldn't have to do housework.

In addition to being spoiled, I was also becoming rebellious. My father was still a strong influence in my house despite his deteriorating sickness. Though my mother and sisters fawned over me when I was little, as I grew older I started to resent the fact my father was in a wheel chair and not able to take me places or do things with. I started to feel sorry for myself and began to act out. I began to hang out more with my friends on the corner and became less and less interested in what was happening at home.

When I entered the fourth grade at Saint Anthony's I met a boy who would become one of my best friends throughout my life. He moved to Florida after eighth grade graduation but was the kind of friend you don't always have to be with in order to keep that special bond. When we see each other, even today, after years of absence, we talk as if we had just seen each other the day before. Luke's background was the opposite of mine. In his family there were three boys and one girl. He was the oldest in his family and the youngest of his siblings was a girl.

Even though our backgrounds were different, we shared a lot of the same interests. We both had a fondness for literature and adventure movies. Movies that showed clear-cut battles between good and evil: John Wayne Westerns, Errol Flynn adventures, Gary

Cooper's stoic portrayals and Henry Fonda's inspirational elegance. It wasn't star worship that inspired us. It was the belief in and respect for the characteristics they portrayed and the history they idealized.

Luke shared those interests and together we would seek out the classics, read them, understand them, and strive to emulate them. I think we were the only fourth graders who had read Homer's *Iliad* and "*Odyssey*. The heroes of those stories leapt off the pages and entered my soul: Achilles, Hector, Ajax, Ulysses, Particles, Paris, and all the others. They displayed all the attributes I believed were noble and uncovered the true essence of our humanity: courage, loyalty, friendship, perseverance, duty, honesty, self-sacrifice, faith and patriotism.

We were also both very interested in girls and by some wonderment they were interested in us. Into our little group we added two more who became our fast friends, Jim and Pat. By the time fifth grade came around the four of us were firmly entrenched as the top of the in crowd. We even started an exclusive club called the "Four Aces." Luke was the ace of spades, Pat was the ace of diamonds, Jim was the ace of hearts and I was the ace of clubs. Luke and I attracted the attention of the two hottest girls in our class. This was in a more innocent time when seventh and eighth graders were not having sex. It was enough to get together and go roller skating, go to a movie or play pee-wee golf. The heavy make outs and petting would not come until high school.

So it was under these circumstances that I was growing up. Socially I was being positively reinforced by my peers, at home I was virtually put on a pedestal by my family and yet the loss of my father's mobility and a sense of his deteriorating health I started feeling sorry for myself and as a result became increasingly more rebellious.

Although my father had the mental capacity at that time to discipline me and try to teach me what was right, he didn't have the physical ability to back it up. As a result I took full advantage of the situation. By the time I graduated from eighth grade I had pretty much established my personality. Whatever group I was with pretty much did what I wanted to do. Through my self-confidence and native intelligence I was mostly able to convince my friends to go along with me. When it came to picking teams to play baseball or football at Palmer Park or Morandis Field or at the end of the street in front of the Edison Plant I would often be one of the captains that did the picking.

I had a successful academic record from Saint Anthony's grammar school; such a good record that although I wanted to go to Fenger High School, a co-ed public school, the nuns and priests approached my parents and strongly suggested that I go to Mendel Catholic College Preparatory High School. It was from this incident that I finally realized how poor we were. Due to a long string of union strikes and basically not having good benefits to begin with, my father had been left with virtually no health care. My sisters, Jo, Prudy and Kathy had gotten jobs immediately upon turning sixteen and each one gave their entire check to my parents. My parents, in turn, would give them an allowance. This continued throughout the time that my father was alive.

Each of my sisters went to work at IBM after graduating from high school and continued to give my parents their checks. I don't know what our family would have done without them. Is it any wonder that they became my heroes? Eventually Kathy got married but Jo and Prudy remained single and continued to support the family. So when my parents were besieged with requests to send me to Mendel they refused, saying that they could not afford it. My sisters had gone to Saint Willobroad, the less expensive Catholic co-ed high school. In order to get me to go to the all-male Mendel the delegation offered to help subsidize my education by fund-raising and using parish money. My father ultimately agreed to send me, and though it would be a great financial burden to my family, my father declined the financial assistance.

I started out brilliantly at Mendel but I eventually abused the privilege I had been given. Mendel was divided into sections. Freshman-year classes started with sections, one and two of which were "Honor Sections." Sections three and four were "Academic Sections" and downward accordingly. I started in section two, which offered algebra,

Latin, biology and the services of the best Augustinian and lay teachers. I quickly found out, however, that most of my friends were in the lower sections or had gone to Fenger and year by year through cutting classes, goofing off and not studying, I eventually graduated at the bottom of my class.

While my academic career was going down in flames, my social life was red hot. Once again through my self-confidence and not through good looks, I was basically dating any girl I chose. As I mentioned there wasn't much actual sex going on but the encounters were becoming more intense. The girls back then pretty much understood that they controlled the situation with one little word, "NO!"

The part of Roseland I lived in was called "Bum Town." The IC (Illinois Central) train station on 115th and Front streets was the last Chicago stop on the far south side othe city. It was at this stop that indigents would hop off the railroad cars and set up their camps. Back then, before the days of political correctness, indigents and homeless people were referred to as "bums." Most of this practice had stopped before I was old enough to experience it, but the name stuck.

Being about as far south as you could go and still remain in Chicago while also being east of Michigan Avenue made you feel left out of the hustle and bustle of the city.

Although the Loop was only about fifteen miles away, it might have been in the next state. "Going downtown" was an event that took special preparation. If you chose to ride the IC train you usually planned to get off at the Randolph Street Station. This would put you in the heart of downtown with easy access to the large, ornately decorated theatres like the Michael Todd, the State Lake, The Oriental, and the Chicago Theatre. You would also have to pick out an affordable restaurant to go to before or after the show. Of course, all of this would have to be coordinated with the train schedule and your limited budget.

The excitement and obvious affluence of that great city, evidenced by the skyscrapers, glass buildings, and crowded streets, was in direct contrast with my surroundings. Bum Town was definitely not a slum. It could, however, in the strictest definition of the word, be what was known as a ghetto. A ghetto is merely a neighborhood or area made up almost exclusively of the same type of people from the same background, same economic condition and shared values. Bum Town was defined as an Italian-American working-class neighborhood that believed in family, education, hard work, self-sacrifice and the promise of America. If they could not realize the American Dream in their lifetime, they would work their whole life to insure that their children could attain it.

Even though the old-timers were proud of their Italian heritage, they insisted that their children learn English and immerse themselves in the customs and traditions of this land of opportunity. They took education very seriously and paid close attention to what was going on in the classrooms by checking report cards and attending meetings with the nuns and priests. They were members of such religious community organizations as The Holy Name Society, The Knights of Columbus, The Saint Therese Society and The Blue Army (dedicated to the Virgin Mother).

Bum Town had a lot of apartments, mostly two and four flats and a scattering of wooden houses. Sprinkled throughout were grocery stores, dry cleaners, drug stores, and taverns. There was also a small movie theatre, a bowling alley and a pool hall, most of which were owned by Italians. I can still smell the aroma of cheese, garlic and peppers that greeted you when you entered Spigallone's Italian Grocery Store. There were wooden bins stocked with pasta: mostaccioli, Fussily, shells, linguini, rigatoni, ravioli and more. You could further treat your senses by walking across the street and inhaling the heavenly scent of freshly baked bread and the hot dough that was being prepared at Torino's Bakery.

It was a wonderful place to grow up. There was a strong sense of belonging and a comforting feeling that people were looking out for you. The fact that we hadn't much money didn't bother us. No one else we knew had much money either.

As I grew older, the neighborhood started to change. A lot of the first generation immigrants began to die off and some of their offspring, looking for the better life they had been taught to pursue, started moving to places west of Michigan Avenue. Some of the more adventurous ones were moving even further west to some of the new suburbs that were starting to spring up.

Although the majority of people were still of Italian descent, people with more diverse backgrounds started moving in. As the new residents made their ascent and people left their old homes, the laws of supply and demand established themselves as they always do. When the families who had originally been too poor to live in better areas became more affluent and moved on, those who were making their way up the economic scale were leaving their impoverished countries and communities to start their rise through the American Dream of home ownership and security. Those of us who remained in Bum Town became somewhat territorial. We would hang out on a corner, usually in front of Pat & Mat's soda fountain or in Sam's Pool Room. We didn't cause trouble in our own neighborhood. We knew almost everyone who lived there and many of them were relatives or paisons (people who came from the same area of the old country, or literally, countrymen).

At the same time we didn't want anyone else starting any trouble there either. Most of the time, the mere presence of ten or fifteen guys hanging around together would be a deterrent to outsiders with mischief in mind but sometimes we would find ourselves outnumbered or alone. Those times usually ended up in a beating followed by an attempt at revenge. We would gather up our numbers and if we knew who the perpetrators were, we would visit them in their neighborhoods and pay them back in kind. This was a different period of time. We did not fight over drugs or criminal control of anything. There were gangs—the "Bum Town Gents," "The Top Hats," and "The Deuces," to name a few—but they were mostly innocent compared to the violence of today. They were tough, but there was hardly ever a fight involving the use of weapons, or even any serious injuries.

 I never acted like a bully. I would not go out to consciously start a fight; in fact, I would usually try to talk my way out of one. However, if I found myself in a situation in which I could not avoid one, or if someone was picking on a defenseless person, I would generally react. Unfortunately I wasn't always the victor in such circumstances. One evening I was challenged to a fight by a boy from outside my neighborhood. He was not happy about my going out with his girlfriend. And he would not be persuaded that I had no idea she was his girlfriend. The end result of that exchange for me was a broken nose and a call to my sister to come and pick me up.

 On another particular evening some of the younger guys from our neighborhood went to a dance in an area that was the home base of a gang on West 95th Street. They were beaten up pretty badly and warned never to return. They drove down to Bum Town and found two of my friends and me sitting on a stoop in front of Saint Anthony's Church, drinking some beer, and told us what happened. I could see by their torn clothes and bruises that they had been hit pretty hard. We followed the younger boys back to the scene of the confrontation. As we turned a corner their car stopped in front of five youths walking down the middle of the street. Their car doors opened and they got out. When it first happened, the other young people were taken back. Once they recognized the occupants, however, they smiled and started walking forward. They hadn't noticed our car so when we also came out, four of them ran away. The one who stood his ground stared at us as we surrounded him. I told the others to stay back and rushed at him. When it was over, he had a bloody nose but when I knew he was beat I left him on the street with no further injuries. I told him that he and his friends were to leave our guys alone or we would be back.

    In scenarios like these I believed I was emulating my heroes of literature and the movies. I would strive to control my weaker impulses but I would not be intimidated or stand by while those who were weaker were oppressed or taken advantage of. I would always strive to live on the better side of my humanity. Many years after I got back from Vietnam someone asked me why I would go ten thousand miles away to fight for people I didn't know. I looked at him and said that I didn't know him that well, either, but if I saw someone breaking into his house and threatening to kill him and his family, I would hope I would try to help. He looked at me like I was from another planet and I knew I could never explain it to him.

As my high school years were coming to an end the natural thing to start thinking about was college. If my parents were wise they would have backed my sisters' academic careers to the hilt instead. As it was, the girls were not encouraged to go to college. Upon graduating high school each one applied to and was hired by IBM. Jo and Prudy each had a twenty-five year career and retired with good benefits. Kathy, the youngest, stayed there for sixteen years until she left to rear her children. My first real job after I got home from Vietnam was also with IBM, so at one time all four of us were employed by the corporate giant. Jo was an executive secretary, Prudy was in accounts receivable and handled such major customers as Sears and Kathy was in charge of a field engineering education unit. They were well respected and when they left IBM they were much sought after.

As I mentioned, all the family attention was directed on me to go to college. I felt the pressure as soon as I entered high school and I understood the importance of it. My family needed me to help out not only financially, but also by being the male to head the family due to my father's debilitating illness. Instead,

I reacted to the pressure by being rebellious and irresponsible. Since there was no one who could physically restrain me I started staying out late, drinking and not coming home for days at a time. I was in constant motion, not wanting to stop to reflect on my responsibilities. Since most of my friends had intact families with fathers willing and able to crack heads, they had curfews and restrictions that I did not have. As a result I started hanging out with the seedier and older group in the neighborhood. This gave me an even greater standing with the boys and girls my age. It was starting to become a situation where a girl who dated me was either envied or had her reputation ruined, depending on which group she was with.

    I started working at the age of fifteen as a soda jerk at a neighborhood soda fountain, but unlike my sisters I was able to keep the money I made without giving anything to my family. My father used to say that "a boy has to have some spending money on him." Unfortunately the soda fountain at which I worked was connected to a bar where mostly older Italians came to drink grappa and smoke stogies. It was eventually brought up to my family that this was not a good environment for a young boy.

    After that I was a bag boy at the old National Tea grocery store and from there I went on to work a few summers at the Sherwin Williams paint factory. While at Sherwin Williams I did give some money to my family, but not to the extent that my sisters did.

During this time my mother was becoming more and more frustrated with me. While she was constantly asking for more help and responsibility from me, my father was telling her not to be so hard on me. It was getting to the point that she was being called in to my school often after I had been suspended for some infraction. She was becoming so frustrated and angry with my lack of help around the house that she would cause the priests to reverse their roles and automatically come around to defending me. It would start with the Augustinian disciplinarian saying, "Now Mrs. Lofrano, Chuck is not really a bad boy." My mother would interrupt and say, "Oh, Father, yes he is. He doesn't come home! I can't leave his father and go out! He doesn't help!" etc., etc.

Her nickname for me became "Bastard." When I would come home after days of absence she would yell, "Well, well, the Bastard's home!" She would pack my bags, put them on the dining room table and tell me to leave. Of course I knew I could never have it any better than I had it there so I just refused to leave. Sometimes she would lock me out of the house and continued to do so until some neighbors would ask her why her son was found sleeping in the yard as they made their way to work in the morning.

When I think of my mother now I remember a loving, self-sacrificing woman who dedicated her life to her husband and her children. I know that in a way she was directing her frustration and sorrow for her stricken husband to her no-account spoiled son and I gave her plenty of justification. In later years we became very close and it's not a coincidence that five of her great-granddaughters have "Rose" as a middle name.

As I mentioned I was popular with girls and went out with quite a few. None of that mattered the day I walked into a restaurant on 103rd Street and Halsted Avenue. There, in the back of the restaurant was the most beautiful girl I had ever seen. Pam was the embodiment of every fantasy I ever had. Her face was perfectly shaped and she had rich brown eyes, long thick eyelashes and full expressive lips. She was tall and slim, and had full, long, luxuriant brown hair. It took my breath away just to look at her. It seemed she wasn't paying much attention to me. Actually I had come to the restaurant to see some other girls I met and I asked them who the girl in the back of the restaurant was. When I found out her name I was shocked. It seemed she was the younger sister of two girls I knew. Suzanne was going out with my friend Dennis DeYoung. Suzanne was a stunningly beautiful girl and had a sister named Christine who had expressed interest in going out with me. Christine was also beautiful but for some reason we never got together. I knew the family had two beautiful girls but I had no idea the most beautiful of all was still to be revealed to me.

☆ ☆ ☆

Before I get into my courtship of Pam, allow me to backtrack to the days of music. The arrival of the Beatles in America was like a category five hurricane, a tsunami and an earthquake registering a nine on the Richter scale, all in one. It not only changed the music scene forever but the social scene as well. Almost every young male who watched the *Ed Sullivan Show* secretly dreamed of learning an instrument and joining a band. It hit some of us who were already playing instruments harder and with more urgency to seek out others to form a group good enough to perform.

I had been taking lessons on the tenor saxophone and the clarinet for several years, and after the Beatles debut I sought out others who were into music. In my neighborhood I didn't know any guitar players. It seems that coming out of the fifties, we were playing horns, drums and accordions. I formed a trio with me on the sax, a drummer and an accordion player. We played for some teen clubs and dances but our bread and butter was weddings. There were no disc jockeys spinning records in those days. Live bands were the order of the day, and at the age of fifteen I could make fifty to one hundred dollars plus my tips for just a few hours work on a Saturday night. I could have as much alcohol and food as I wanted as well as the attention of the young girls in attendance.

✩ ✩ ✩

Further west and north on 101st and State Street a Chicago legend was being made: Dennis DeYoung walked across the street there to the home of John and Chuck Panozzo, my first cousins, and asked if they wanted to practice together. John played the drums, Chuck played the guitar and Dennis played the accordion. Later, they got a lead guitarist and formed the group, "Trade Winds" which turned into "TW4," which evolved into "Styx," which sold tens of millions of records. The reason I bring this up is that this period is very important to me. My playing continued to contribute to my sense of confidence and accomplishments and the success of Dennis allowed me to continue to believe that great success is available to those who are willing to dream and work hard.

So I knew Suzanne through Dennis and Christine but the most beautiful sister, Pamela Joy, I had yet to meet. After the first time I saw her in the restaurant on Halsted I could not get her out of my mind. I would think of her every day and dream about her every night. My experience with most girls up to that time was that I would meet them, call them, go out with them and then drop them when some one I thought was better came along. It was all in my control because quite frankly, I didn't much care. This, however, was very different. I started to doubt myself and wondered what would happen if she turned me down. The amazing thing about Pam was that she didn't realize how beautiful and desirable she was so she tended to seem overly flirtatious. I think she felt she had some power over men but I don't think she fully understood the deep effect she had on men of all ages, or where her innocent flirtations might lead. While other classically beautiful women gave off an aura of aloofness, Pam seemed totally approachable, shining her charms and beauty on princes and peasants alike.

The next week I called her to ask her out. Her father had gone to California to investigate the job and housing situation there in anticipation of an eventual move. As a result her mother was in charge of the family and doing her best to keep things going and protect her three beautiful daughters as well as the two other children, a younger boy and a four-year-old girl. Due to this situation Pam was not allowed to go out on dates, especially with boys her mother did not know. To get around this I suggested that I drive by her neighborhood, pick her up and take her to McDonald's and then we could just hang around her house. This continued for some weeks until her mother got to know me better. Suzanne told her I was John and Chuck's cousin and her mother was familiar with my aunt and uncle through Dennis and the band. This put her more at ease and she finally relented and allowed us to date. Soon we were going steady and I devoted most of my free time to being with Pam.

Then, all of a sudden it was over. The day came when her family was called by their father to move to California. I was devastated. Suzanne was older and seriously involved with Dennis so she was allowed to stay in Chicago with her grandmother. Pam, however, was to move with the rest of the family. Pam and I followed her family in my car to O'Hare Airport, where I watched her board the plane and continued watching while the plane lifted off. I drove back in silence not even turning on the radio. It took me a few days to leave the house and I tried hard to put her out of my mind. Some of the ways I tried were to increase my drinking, seeing more girls and staying out even later than before. My exploits starting getting bolder.

One night two of my new nefarious friends and I decided that we would steal a car. I had been cruising around Pam's old neighborhood as I was wont to do those days and passed a really sharp-looking convertible. The car looked familiar but the beer I had been drinking clouded any recognition. After spotting the car and deciding that was the one, we stopped at a gas station where one of my friends got out to buy a screwdriver and some other things he said he needed to pop the ignition and start the car. I had no idea what we were going to do with the car if we did manage to steal it but that didn't matter.

We drove out to our destination and John and I got into the convertible while Wayne got behind the wheel of my car. As soon as we got the convertible started lights went on and we heard loud voices from the house that the car was in front of. We pulled out just as three men were coming down the stairs. As John drove the car I looked back to see the men getting into a car and start to chase us. We sped down the street pushing the convertible as fast as it could go; luckily, that was pretty fast. As we drove up 103rd Street we noticed that a train was nearing a crossing. As the gates came down we knew it was now or never so John pressed the pedal as far as it would go, closed his eyes and the car flew through the crossing just as the gate was closing behind us. We quickly jumped out of the convertible and got into my car which had come back to get us. I'm sure the sound of the freight surging behind us muted the expletives of our pursuers. As we drove away, my head cleared a little and I suddenly realized whose car it was that we had chosen. It belonged to the brother of a girl that I knew quite well, a first-rate body builder with the body to prove it. He was also a good guy and to this day I strongly regret my foolish actions.

I was never proud of this incident, but when word got out that I had stolen a car and not been caught, younger kids from the neighborhood started looking up to me for the wrong reasons. When one of these kids who went to Mendel was caught for stealing a car, he told the priest that he had learned his trade from me. That prompted another visit to the school for my mother who once again recited her then famous "He's no good" speech.

In 1967, my senior year and the year before Pam left, the neighborhood and Mendel were going through integration pains. It seemed that at least once a day there was a fight behind the gym between one white and one black student or sometimes between several whites and blacks. I had a pretty good reputation as someone you would not want to intentionally mess with but I had never taken part in any of the racial strife. One particular afternoon a group of white students starting circling a small group of black students, who were doing nothing more than talking and smoking cigarettes. I was off to the side with a group of my friends and recognized the leader of the white kids, my friend Andy, then saw one of my black friends in the circle. As the whites were about to make their move I called out to Andy and approached the group, causing them to stop their advance. I walked up to Andy, put my arm around him and asked him for a cigarette. When he handed me his pack I quietly told him that the guys in the circle were friends of mine and I'd appreciate it if they'd leave them alone. Andy smiled and said, "Sure man, no problem," and disbanded the group. I could see my friend Reggie watching me from inside the circle of black kids. He gave me a quick nod, got up and went back to his classes.

I thought no more about this incident until a few weeks later. Pam, her sister Christine, a friend of mine and I were on a double date in Chicago's Old Town. It was very late and we were walking to the dimly lit parking lot where I had left my car. All of a sudden I saw a group of about ten black youths coming towards us. They started to slowly fan out to where they would have us surrounded when they reached us. I truly believed we were going to get seriously hurt so I pushed Pam behind me against a chain link fence. Just as the group got to our side of the street I heard one of them say, "Hey, Chuck, how you doin'?" I strained my eyes in the darkness and barely recognized Reggie. Whether he recognized me at that instant or had known it was me all along I never bothered to ask. I vigorously shook his hand and told him in all honesty how truly happy I was to see him.

At the insistence of my father I finally entered Wilson Junior College, about the only school I could get into due to my horrendous academic record from Mendel. This was during the time when things were spinning out of control in my neighborhood. Drugs were making their way into the community, and several of my friends on the street were going down the tube very quickly. Joey Jay was shot twice in the stomach over a bad drug deal. Filo became a "three-time loser" when he was caught trying to rob a gas station. so he was going away for a long time. Jerry had been hit by a train while he was drunkenly walking close to the tracks and was barely hanging on to his life.

My half-hearted endeavors at Wilson as well as my social life were not fulfilling and I knew I had to do something. At this time I started thinking long and hard about the war that was raging in Vietnam. I had grown up with strong feelings of duty and patriotism, and had studied history closely and recognized the intrinsic evils of socialism and communism. My immigrant grandparents had fled a socialist society that was rigid in its lack of opportunities to rise above the station of your father. Communism was even worse. It robbed your soul and demanded that its people serve the state to the exclusion of all human rights, needs, wants and desires. It created slaves, people whose lives were controlled by a few elites deeming themselves superior to the masses.

I started seriously to think about joining the service. The first and only choice I came to was the United States Marine Corps. To me they were the "Knights of the Round table," the "Three Hundred Spartans ", "Rogers Rangers," the "Few and the Proud." If I were going to fight a war it would be as a marine. Somewhere deep inside of me I knew I needed the hard discipline that the marines could provide. Although I knew my family loved me dearly, I also knew they didn't have the power to keep my wilder inclinations in check. Before my life, blessed with all the opportunities and potential given to me by the generations that went before me, went down the tubes, I had to do something to save myself.

The war was not as vilified at that time as it was to become shortly. It was only during the days when young men were living in fear of being drafted that the protests were the largest and loudest. It is interesting to note that the protests died down just as President Nixon ended the draft.

For these reasons in addition to a yearning for my passage into manhood, I decided to join the marines. I knew it would break my father's heart but I felt it was very important to me. I could literally see a life of failure and disappointment ahead of me if I didn't change. Things had been pretty easy for me so far in my life. I did whatever I wanted to do with not much restriction but I could feel I was running out of time. The older I got, the more important my decisions were becoming and the harsher the consequences were for the stupid ones.

When I thought of the tough discipline that was the reputation of the Marine Corps, I knew I would benefit from it. This, plus the honest love and duty I felt for this country, the land that my grandparents had come to, the land that gave my family the opportunity to pursue their dreams, this country was worth fighting for. I have never second-guessed my decision.

On a clear frosty morning in November of 1967, I walked up to the recruiting offices on

Michigan Avenue. The clean-cut, bright-eyed marine recruiter started to give his pitch when I put up my hand and quietly said, "Where do I sign?" His look of surprise quickly vanished, giving way to a warm smile. He gave me my options. The United States Marines Corps normally required a four-year enlistment but, due to the need for marines in Vietnam, they were offering a two-year deal. If you chose the two-year deal you were pretty much assured that you were going to Vietnam. I signed delayed enlistment papers, which meant that although I signed in November of 1967, I didn't have to report for three months but would get credit for those three months regardless. With the tour for marines in Vietnam being thirteen months, plus the three-month credit, I'd only have eight months left after my tour. It sounded like a good deal at the time and I signed the papers.

That night, as always, my family sat down to dinner. This night I made sure I was in attendance. Dinnertime was very special to my family. It was not only a time to partake of the delicious meals my mother made with care and love, it was also a time for conversation. As I think back now I truly regret those days I was not present for that very pleasant ritual. My sisters would discuss their day at work and my father would listen attentively, truly interested in what was being said. You could tell he was enjoying the world through their eyes. Every once in a while they would stop and ask his opinion on something and he would beam while he offered his advice. However, on this particular night it was I who brought discourse into this normally pleasant tableau.

When the dessert and coffee had been served and all were seated again I announced the news that on that day I had joined the United States Marine Corps. There was dead silence. I looked closely at my father's eyes as he sat at the head of the table in his wheelchair, and could sense the conflicting emotions running through him. There was a sadness and profound sense of fear as I am sure all parents feel at a moment like this, but at the same time there was a sense of pride that his son, his youngest child, had made such a decision. He asked me if I were sure this was what I wanted. He reminded me I could still get a college deferment and he had been told that since I was the only son and he was disabled I could also apply for a hardship deferment. I explained that I had thought it all through and I was sure this was what I wanted. I walked over to him, hugged him, kissed him on the cheek and told him I was sorry. I assured him I would be all right then turned to hug my mother and sisters.

They would tell me later that my father would eat his dinner in the front room off a snack tray in front of the television. He would follow the progress of the first televised war in hopes of hearing the whereabouts and exploits of the 1st Marine Division of which I was a part. They also told me that on the day the marine in dress blues came to inform my family that

I was wounded, my mother would not open the door while my father was shouting to let him in. My sisters had been called home from work and soon my home was filled with family, friends and neighbors in an effort to console my parents and lend their support and love.

Now I was flying back to the warmth and support I so desperately looked forward to. I had left a haven of peace, love and comfort and spent what seemed like a lifetime in hell. I learned that life was fragile and could not be taken for granted. There were many lessons that I learned that I was not quite cognitive of at the time. I was just concentrating on getting back to my home. My base of strength, where I hoped to heal physically and, if I was fortunate, to heal my soul.

CHAPTER FIVE

Back in the World

Glenview, Illinois
November,1968

    We touched down at the Glenview Naval Air Station on a clear fall day. We made a brief stopover in Fairbanks, Alaska but with the medications I was on I was restricted to my rack on the C-130. I was still in a semi-conscious state as they carried me off the plane on a stretcher, but even in this condition I was filled with such euphoria that I might as well have been flying off the plane on my own power. The air was crisp and clean, in direct contrast to the fetid stench of the jungle and the oppressive humidity that weighed down on you like a giant rock . Also missing were the smells of dung fires, napalm, cordite and blood.
    I drifted off to sleep and woke in a bed with sold, crisp white sheets. I was in an immaculate ward with perfectly lined up racks filled with young men, This was the Great Lakes Naval Hospital. On first take it was vastly different from the naval hospital in Japan. Those of us who got this far had been pretty much worked on and cleaned up. Most of the patients here had been stabilized but still needed further attention and further surgeries. There were amputees who would be given therapy, prosthetics and rehabilitation. I was to have several more operations on my nerves. One

of the procedures was to shorten my arm to help re-attach the severed nerves. Another was to put a permanent plate in my wrist and still another was to insert a rod in my arm to reinforce my shattered bone.

When I was shot, the round had severed the nerves in my arm and my hand had snapped shut into a fist that I was unable to open. The day after I got to Great Lakes I was scheduled to have Kirschner wires attached to my cast, a device that started from the top of the cast beneath the knuckles, came out straight and then arched up like a hook. From the hook dangled five small finger slings, in which my fingers were to be placed, thereby forcing them to spread out and lift, opening the hand. I would also be scheduled for therapy to loosen the joints in my fingers, exercise the hand and try to increase the use of my arm and hand.

That next day after I returned from the Kirschner procedure, I found two people waiting for me. I had graduated with Tom from Mendel and I knew Cary from Chicago and ITR at Camp Pendleton in California. I had no idea that Tom had enlisted in the marines and was really happy to see Cary. I hadn't realized that they had been to Vietnam let alone been wounded. Tom had received severe shrapnel in his shoulder and lost some mobility. Cary had actually been wounded twice, once accidently by our own troops and once in a fierce close hand-to-hand battle. Cary had remained on his feet after a grenade shattered the bones in his leg until the battle was over. He collapsed right after the last shot was fired and after several operations would still walk with a pronounced limp until the day he died, which, unbeknownst to us, was only a few short years away.

Life was good. I was back in the "World." I had reunited with two friends from my previous life who had shared my experiences. I felt that I was on the way to recovery and my family had come to see me. The only thing that would make this better was Pam. I had never stopped thinking about her constantly. I had seen her while I was in California before I left for Vietnam, reuniting when I was at San Onofre and I stayed with her and her family several times at their home in Solana Beach. We spent the day together with some of my marine friends and several of her girlfriends that I also knew who were visiting her from Chicago. She drove me back to Staging right before I shipped out and during the time we spent together in California I asked her to marry me. Since she had more sense than I did she said no. She said we were too young and the future was too uncertain.

When I called my family to tell them when I was coming home I asked my sister Prudy to tell Pam what had happened and that I would be okay. I also told her not to have Pam contact me. I asked her to tell Pam I would contact her when I had more information. At that time the outcome of my condition was less clear than it became later. I was still in fear of having my arm amputated or totally incapacitated. As always, when it came to Pam my confidence was shaky. Pam had so much to offer: beauty, intelligence, kindness and personality. I felt that to offer her anything less than perfection would be an insult. I was torn between needing to see her and not wanting her to see me in my disabled condition. Later on she would try to call me from California to see how I was doing. Like an immature child I would tell the corpsman to tell her I was not in the ward. I knew that if I heard her voice I would be in agony.

In spite of missing Pam, it was a truly magical day when my family had arrived to see me. My father was in his wheelchair and there were my sisters, mother and several aunts, uncles and cousins. It was a tearful but happy reunion and we were joined by Tom and Cary. I could feel my heart start to heal as I was reunited with the people who had nurtured me and supported me unconditionally through the good things and the bad. All parent/child conflicts of the past melted away and I felt safe and redeemed in their love. I wasn't ready to tell them what their son, brother and nephew had seen and done. I didn't know if I would ever be able to tell them. It was enough for now to try to believe that my life was on its way back to normalcy not realizing there is no such thing as a normal life.

Soon after the family reunion a great revelation came over me. When I was with my family I was a son, a brother, a nephew, a cousin, a man who had been reared to believe in God, to not hurt others and to be kind and respectful. How could someone brought up this way undergo the horrors of war? I was sure this was the same in all wars. In addition to the training we received, I believe there is an unconscious psychological trick we employ without ever realizing it. I remember it from watching countless war movies and personally experiencing it in Vietnam. It was the use of nicknames. In Vietnam I was known as "Dago," and served with and knew guys whose names were Red, Moon, Polack, Four Eyes, Doc, Chief and Whitey. I was sure the subconscious thinking was that Chuck Lofrano, who came from a good family, could not be doing the things that had to be done in combat. To keep your sanity you almost had to believe that someone else was doing these things. It was a façade, a mask put up to protect one's psyche. Sometimes it worked and sometimes it didn't.

Time passed quickly at Great Lakes. It was during this time that I met Tim. I was in between operations. Tom, Cary and I had added a few fellow patients to our circle. We became a pretty salty group. We would sit around telling war stories while not trying to think about what we would do after our hospital stay. We were becoming infamous in our ward for our constant harassing of the navy staff. Our fame became legend throughout the hospital after we organized a sit-down strike in front of

Captain Alice Wallace's office to protest the suspension of our phone privileges.

Earlier that week we had staged wheelchair races down the main hallway of our floor. It was quite an event, with bets coming in from all over. We probably would have gotten away with it except for the long, ugly, dark, rubber skid marks on the navy's immaculately scrubbed floor. The punishment for our "Wheelchair 500 Race" was to have no phone rights for two weeks. After a two-day sit-in, a thorough scrubbing of the floor and a promise never to repeat the event, we were reprieved.

One day, as we were plotting how to sneak down to the Rathskellar restaurant to get some contraband pizza, a nurse approached us pushing a lanky, hollow-eyed, sandy-haired figure in a Wicker wheelchair. The nurse introduced us to him as Tim and, with a wink, asked us not to corrupt him. Tim was very quiet. He answered the obligatory questions of what unit, where stationed, and where he was hit. The rest of the time he would just sit and stare. He was always with us and seemed to enjoy our company, but for the most part he remained silent and introspective.

One morning at about 3:00 I was awakened by someone gently pushing on my shoulder. I awoke with a start and as I focused I saw the gaunt expressionless eyes of Tim staring at me. He asked if I would go to the head with him for a cigarette. After lights out it was against the rules to smoke in the head but they were pretty lenient about it as long as we didn't abuse the privilege. I sensed that Tim wanted to unload something. For days I had felt he wanted to talk but didn't know how to start. For some reason, on this morning he chose to reveal his story. After the cigarettes were lit and a few deep inhales were accomplished Tim began.

He was a marine grunt as were most of us in the ward. Tim was an 0331 M60 Infantry Machine Gunner, as was I, which might explain why he chose me as his audience. Veterans feel comfortable talking about the war with other veterans, and more comfortable with veterans of their own branch of service and most comfortable with those who shared their MOS, (Military Occupational Specialty)

Tim's unit had been responsible for a series of villages in Quang Nam Province. The villages were designated as friendly, so the unit's main purpose was as a show of force and a discouragement to the VC in the area. Whenever they passed one particular village, however, they always drew fire from some of the hooches. They took casualties constantly but were always ordered not to return fire lest they hit civilians. After literally weeks of being pinned down and taking casualties their lieutenant had enough. On that fateful morning as the first squad passed abreast of the village a stronger than usual barrage of automatic fire erupted. Their radio man caught some rounds in the head and Tim remembered seeing the lieutenant being spattered in the face with the dead man's blood. The lieutenant ordered Tim and his gun team to open fire on the offending hooches. No one needed to be told twice. They immediately opened up and then, on file, rushed the village with two platoons.

Tim had concentrated his fire on one hooch and had emptied three one hundred-round belts of 7.62 rounds into its yielding walls of straw and bamboo. When his gun team entered the hooch they saw in the middle of the floor sprawled out in gruesome shapes of twisted limbs and lying in pools of blood, three young men in black pajamas. The AK-47s lying around them gave proof that they in fact were VC. As Tim surveyed the rest of the hooch he noticed a table of bamboo in the corner. He said a sickening feeling came over him as he slowly walked to the scene. When he pushed the table aside he saw something that shook him to the very depths of his soul. It's hard to tell the age of a woman whose face has been erased by machine gun fire, but Tim figured she was probably in her mid-twenties. The ages of the two children lying next to her were easier to discern. Tim had nephews back in the world who were two and four, so he was sure that's how old these children were.

He remained silent for a long time after he related this experience to me. I was sure it was the first time he had talked about it and had a strong sense that he wasn't quite finished, but there was no way I was going to press him or break in on his thoughts. He looked at me with tears in his eyes and asked me if I thought people would understand. I remember saying something innocuous like, "It was war. You didn't know those civilians were inside and it was the VC's fault for using them as shields." I told him people would understand and forgive him and he should forgive himself.

The last time I heard of Tim was ten years after that. It had taken four policemen with mace to subdue him in a neighborhood tavern.

There were many horror stories of how we were treated when we got home. On some flights servicemen were cautioned to remove their uniforms before they landed lest they be ridiculed or spat upon by their contemporaries who had stayed at home. There were some misguided miscreants who threw eggs and bags of excrement at them. Some college students would get a hold of the names and phone numbers of those killed in Vietnam and call their families telling them how happy they were that their sons and fathers had been killed by the heroic soldiers of Vietnam.

I knew that stories like Tim's could and would be taken out of context by those who wanted to discredit us and the war. Tim didn't start that day looking for innocent civilians to kill. The enemy had learned that it was to their advantage to use innocent civilians to hide behind and the anti-war movement was always ready to jump on any excuse to further justify their own cowardice and agenda. Rather than blame the communists for using human shields we were vilified for firing back to save our lives.

These reactions to us were on the lower side of the scale. There were other reactions including bewilderment, fear, misunderstanding and even indifference. Fortunately there was also some happiness and gratitude. This was fostered mostly by family and close friends. When I first came home I was truly blessed. There were red, white and blue banners strung across the light poles of 117th Street reading, "Welcome Home Chuck," and "Chuck For President." The entire block came out to greet me. They cheered and applauded me as I got out of the car and my house was filled with family and friends. My heart almost burst with love, joy and pride as I kissed and hugged the people who had been instrumental in the formation of my character.

In direct contrast to my joyous situation was the reception that the other young marine sitting in the front seat of the car had encountered. Since Cary lived about a half-hour from me my family had offered to take him home. For some reason, no one was home when we dropped Cary off. We waited as he, a full cast on his leg from his toes to his hip, walked around his house on his crutches to try to get in. I finally took him home with me. Although we had been friends before, from that day forward we became as close as two friends could be. Two years later I had asked Cary to be the godfather of my first child. Since he was Jewish and I was Catholic we had to get a dispensation from the church, which meant that Cary had to sign a statement that if something happened to me and my wife, he would see to it that my child would be raised as a Catholic. Tragically, this was never to be.

One dark morning , a few days before my wife gave birth to my first daughter, I was awakened by a frantic knocking on my door. It was Cary's sister crying hysterically and screaming that Cary was dead. He had been killed in a car accident while attending school at Western Illinois University. Cary had started drinking heavily towards the end of his life and he would always ask me "Why weren't we allowed to go into North Vietnam?" Cary was a good, charismatic, and generous man with a great future, and a true friend. When he entered my life I felt uplifted, and his loss will stay with me always.

Cary's wake was a somber affair. We accept the passing of our friends and relatives when they are old. We generally have time to adjust to this inevitability due to a prolonged period of illness or a declared condition with no hope of recovery. It is, however, quite different when death comes to a child or young person. There is a hole left in the universe. The untimely cancellation of the person's future leaves possibilities and questions that can never be answered.

I was told that on the second day of the wake, the sadness was unbearable. Cary had affected many lives as profoundly as he had affected mine. The reason that I had to be told how the wake started that second day was because I was not there. It was on that day that my daughter Deana was born. Deana, the first of my three daughters, and the baby that was to have been Cary's goddaughter. Cary and I had talked about that day many times and he always seemed as pleased as I was at the thought of it.

When Deana was born I called the funeral parlor and asked to speak to Cary's father. His father was overjoyed and said he was coming immediately to the hospital to see the baby. He arrived with his arms filled with roses and chocolates for my wife and thanked her for the "miracle baby." It seemed that the wake had reached its lowest point and the sorrow and despair was crushing. However, when the call came from us and Cary's family announced the birth, there was an instant change of mood. Tears of sadness were immediately replaced with tears of joy. He said that to him it was God's way of showing the continuity of life. One soul leaves the earth and another enters it. He said he knew that Cary was aware of Deana's birth and that he would be at rest.

Two years before Cary's death I had received the last operation I would get at Great Lakes Naval Hospital. The word was passed that because of the influx of patients coming in some of us were to be transferred to the Veterans Administration Hospital on Huron Street in downtown Chicago, otherwise called "VA Lakeside." We were still in the marines so a marine liaison was to be set up for us. Tom and Cary had been released earlier and I was one of the last of my group to go. I had spent three months at Great Lakes and was truly appreciative of the care and concern I received from the highly professional doctors, nurses and corpsmen.

If I counted the field medical hospital unit near Dodge City after first being wounded, I was about to enter my fifth hospital. This facility would prove to be the most interesting of all. For the first time I would be in the minority. Before this I was exclusively with Vietnam veterans and mostly marines. I was now to be in a place that had combat veterans from World War II and Korea from all branches of the services. There was also a large population of servicemen who were not combat veterans but were being cared for by the system.

I was looking forward to talking to the veterans of World War II and Korea. I considered them to be my brothers and had always looked up to them; they, not actors, athletes or politicians, had been my idols. They were the real life embodiment of the great heroic characters of literature that I had come to admire and tried to mold my life after. Guadalcanal, Iwo Jima, Saipan, Midway, D-Day, The Battle of the Bulge, Inchon, Pork Chop Hill: these were magical names that inspired honor, bravery and sacrifice.

As I settled in to my new surroundings and engaged in conversations with my fellow patients I started to realize the extent of how the media, the college campuses and the elitist opinion-makers had been successful in destroying the image of the Vietnam veteran. The overall opinion of most of the older veterans was that we were a whining group of underachieving children who were losing a war against a group of farmers in black pajamas with pitchforks. Eventually, as more of the truth was revealed. these people became strong supporters but at this early stage the media was doing a great job in pushing their propaganda. This was also the reason that Vietnam veterans were not joining organizations like the American Legion and the VFW. We felt unwelcome and unwanted. We knew that we had shared the same experiences in combat that they had. We knew we faced a formidable well trained, well equipped and fierce enemy in the NVA. We knew that although a very small number of troops behaved poorly (as had occurred in all wars from the beginning of time), the vast majority of men who served were honorable, treated women and children with respect and had actually volunteered for combat in Vietnam.

As a matter of fact in the course of the war over a ten year period only twenty-five percent of the forces in Vietnam were draftees as compared to sixty-six percent of the armed forces in World War II. We knew we weren't the bottom of American society without an education as we were being portrayed. Eighty percent of the men who served in Vietnam had a high school education as opposed to sixty-three percent in Korea and forty-five percent in World War II. Seventy-five percent of the men sent to Vietnam had family incomes above the poverty level and fifty percent of these men were from middle income backgrounds. Twenty-three percent of Vietnam Veterans had fathers with professional, managerial or technical jobs.

After the war we found out more facts that negated the lies being presented by the "enlightened ones." *88 percent of the men who actually served in Vietnam were Caucasian, 10% were African American and 1% belonged to other races. 86.% of the men who were killed as a result of hostile action were Caucasian, 12% were Black and 1% belonged to other races*

These were the facts, but the men who chose not to serve had to justify their decision by undermining the reasons, motives and character of those who did. As I stated, much of the truth was not presented back then and as I'm writing this I'm wondering how many people today are totally ignorant of these facts? I don't blame the older veterans for what they thought. I was just saddened and disappointed that they, my heroes, were rejecting us. They had gone to war and returned in a patriotic fervor when even the press was considered a reliable supporter of America and its ideals. Very few people were aware of the turn in the 1960s toward the rejection of traditional values. They didn't know there was a segment of the population that in their arrogance and perceived self-importance felt above reproach.

They were the "all rights" with "no responsibilities" crowd. They believed that if it felt good, do it and by the way, don't you, the unwashed masses dare judge them, the smartest and most privileged people in our society.

*Department of Defense Statistics.

I spent another two months as both an in-patient and out-patient at Lakeside. I had decided to take advantage of the GI Bill and attend the University of Illinois at Chicago Circle campus. One of the most significant things that happened during this time was that Pam came back to Chicago from California. I had heard through her friends that she really did not like California and missed her family and friends in Chicago, but I hadn't heard anything about her returning.

After a night of partying I usually ended up with friends at Tony's Snack Shop on 111th Street and Michigan Avenue. It was a twenty-four-hour restaurant with great food and even better service. One of my running gags was that I would order steak and eggs and, since I couldn't cut the steak due to not being able to use my left arm, my friends would leave the table and I would look around for an attractive girl and ask her for her help. Believe it or not that corny, pathetic scam would usually work and I'd end up with a phone number or, if it worked really well, a ride home for the helpful young lady.

On one particular night I went to Tony's by myself after a night of partying. The restaurant had a main room in front and around the corner there was an additional room to handle the overflow. On this night the restaurant was quite crowded. I looked over the crowd seated at the tables in the front. I gave a cursory nod to some patrons that I recognized but did not know that well. I decided to go to the overflow room to see if any of my friends were there. As I rounded the corner I noticed my friend Dennis, his girlfriend Suzanne and two other members of Styx, which was called Trade Winds at that time. As I approached the table I literally stopped dead in my tracks. As I got close look at their table I noticed there was another girl sitting with her back to me. When she turned around to see who the others were acknowledging I saw that it was Pam. I have no idea what my outward demeanor looked like but inside I was filled with joy and trepidation. I had dreamed of this day for a long time. I longed for it while at the same time dreading it. I had heard from her friends that she had been dating. I had done my best to try to discourage her from having feelings for me due to my disability while at the same time wanting her more than ever. Did she still love me? Had she ever loved me? Was she serious with anyone else? Had she come back for me, or because she missed Chicago and her friends? Those questions and more flashed through my mind as I grabbed a seat next to her. I made some innocuous comments like how great she looked and I was glad to see her. I engaged in this general conversation and found out Dennis and the group had come here after a gig at a local high school dance. During a lull I asked Pam where she was staying and asked if I could take her home. I drove her to her grandmother's, and from that night forward we were inseparable. We were married that next year and started our life in a third-floor apartment on the south side of Chicago.

Left to right; Cary, me, mother Rose, father Sal.

"War is an ugly thing, but not the ugliest of things. The decayed and degraded state of a moral and patriotic feeling which thinks that nothing is worth war is much worse. A man who has nothing for which he is willing to fight – nothing he cares about more than his own safety – is a miserable creature who has no chance of being free, unless made and kept so by the exertions of better men than themselves."

John Stuart Mill

CHAPTER SIX

The Halls of Academia

University of Illinois at
Chicago Circle Campus
1970-1972

I was still undergoing out-patient therapy at Lakeside and receiving disability pay from the Marine Corps. I had been put on temporary retirement but wouldn't be permanently retired from the marines until 1974, four years after I was married. During this time I enrolled at the University of Illinois Chicago Circle Campus. The university was fairly new at that time. It was designed to be a commuter school to handle the large population of Chicago and surrounding areas. Ironically it was built around Halsted and Taylor where my father's family had originally settled when they came to Chicago.

The Jane Adams Hull House still stood as a monument to those early immigrants and reminded me of my family's tales of that place. My uncle Tony Lofrano, who played drums for the David LeWinter Band that performed for many years in the famous Pump Room of the Ambassador East Hotel in Chicago, had first been introduced to music at that facility. My father would go there with his brothers and sisters after school and learn about things like music, sports and cooking.

I decided to major in psychology. I think subconsciously I was trying to understand some of the emotions I was experiencing. Thoughts that ran the gamut of why some would feel compelled to take up arms and defend the rights of others to be free while others felt no such obligation. In combat I wondered why the reactions of men under fire would be so varied. I saw some men cry, laugh, or become wild with anger while some would be utterly emotionless. Why were we affected so differently? I hoped to gain an insight into these events. Unfortunately I found there were no answers in the hallowed halls of academia.

The curricula and main agenda of most of the professors at that time was to blame America first for all the troubles of the world, to hate and revile all our traditions and values and to completely omit the tremendous contributions made by the United States to the countries of the world. There were millions of people who owed their freedom to the United States. We donated billions of dollars in aid and technology to the less fortunate of the world. I have always believed that it is legitimate to bring up and discuss the problems we have had. Slavery had been an abomination in our country and segregation was a disgrace.

The robber barons and the working conditions of the early days of the Industrial Revolution had been intolerable. I also believe that in order to present an atmosphere of learning, a sense of fairness and open minded intellectual honesty, both sides must be presented. The hatred and disdain being heaped upon the United States by these liberal professors omitted such facts as that over six hundred thousand Americans paid for the atrocious sin of slavery in America with their lives. They would never talk about the fact of how millions of people from all over the world were constantly trying to get into the United States by any means possible. They wanted to take advantage of the freedoms and opportunities here as opposed to the Soviet Union style of communism, which most of the professors admired.

Instead of highlighting the many stories of those born in poverty who overcame great odds to become successful, they highlighted those they defined as poor victims. They failed to mention the average poor person in America was still likely to own a car, have a color TV, own a phone, have food to eat and access to an education and job. If any intelligent person would compare our poor people to those of Darfur or Calcutta or Cuba they would find that there was no contest. This was not to say that some people in this country don't deserve help. It's just to point out that opportunity, aid and an education (hopefully not by professors like them) are available to those who wish to take advantage of them. America *has* problems but America is not the problem.

These disseminators of information used to brag that since Castro had taken over Cuba the literacy rate had risen. That was true. What they left out was that children could only read books extolling the virtues of communism, the godlike qualities of Fidel and the evils of capitalism. Any other position was censured and only their point of view was permitted (much like the tactics of these "enlightened" professors). The children of Cuba were told to bury all their individual freedoms and live only for the state. They were taught to turn in their parents if they spoke contrary to the party line and that their miserable living conditions were not the fault of the bankrupt ideology of communism but somehow caused by America.

These "useful idiots" would organize trips to Cuba for their students to view this workers paradise. They were led around by the nose by their "handlers" and shown the phony co-ops that were created strictly for propaganda purposes. They were never allowed to roam around the country without restrictions where they would be able to see the absolute poverty and despair suffered by the Cuban people or the wealth and privilege afforded only to the high party members. To quote George Orwell, "All animals are equal, but some animals are more equal than others."

I would sit in my classes in total bewilderment. We were locked in a cold war with the communists. The differences were clear. Freedom, prosperity and opportunity represented by America and the West versus totalitarianism, subjugation and the loss of humanity as represented by the Soviet Union and Red China. North Korea and Vietnam had been hot battles in this cold war. Russia, the Warsaw Pact and Communist China had armed and supplied their client states to expand their interests and spread their ideology.

The world had settled into what was referred to as a policy of mutual assured destruction. This was to insure that no one would be foolish enough to start a nuclear war, as both sides had the ability to annihilate not only the other side but in fact, destroy the entire planet. As a result, the Soviets started a plan of conquest designed to foster wars in the guise of national movements or civil wars. It was more than obvious to even the most casual observer that these wars were always started with Russian- and Chinese-made weapons, tanks and material. I was in disbelief when I came home and found that the biggest America haters were professors, and journalists. Obviously not everyone in these professions were America-haters but it seemed that it was in these occupations that the hatred was the most pronounced.

There were also some in the religious community and many in the Hollywood establishment that joined with liberal politicians like Ted Kennedy and some Democratic leaders that condemned us and cheered for our enemies as they killed us. Actress "Hanoi Jane" Fonda actually went to North Vietnam and was photographed posing behind an enemy anti-aircraft gun with a huge smile on her face. I guess it made her extremely happy to be sitting behind a communist-made weapon that had most likely killed American servicemen. Other empty headed entertainers made recordings to encourage our enemies and demoralize their fellow countrymen. Many of their hateful words were played to our prisoners of war to tell them that at best they were stupid, and at worst they were war criminals. I did, however, understand the difference between this traitorous behavior and honest dissent.

The singer Joan Baez was an anti-war activist, a Quaker who believed in the tenets of her religion. During Vietnam she condemned the actions of both sides and after the war she condemned the despicable and hideous treatment of the South Vietnamese people by their North Vietnamese "liberators" as well as the three million Cambodians executed by the Pol Pot regime. This was in direct contrast to "Hanoi Jane" vilifying America and giving the enemy the moral right to kill as many of us as possible but being completely silent when it came to the boat people of South Vietnam and the piles of human skulls uncovered in Cambodia.

I had fought communists. When the NVA came south during the Tet Offensive the first ones on their lists marked for assassination were teachers and politicians. When communists took over countries all over the world their targets were newspapers, organized religions and media outlets like radio, television and movies. The orders were to tow the party line or die. Did these America-haters not know this? Did they honestly think that they were so much smarter and more special than everyone else that they could sit with these people and talk them out of things? Did they think that they thought so much like the enemy that they would be considered their comrades? Perhaps they had missed Lenin's explanation of the phrase useful idiots. Perhaps they were absent the day the word "totalitarianism" was taught. Maybe they didn't believe that Joe Stalin had killed fifty million Ukrainians. Maybe they lost count of all the failed five-year plans the Soviet Union had made to bring prosperity to their enslaved people.

The discussions of these topics would be a great opportunity to debate and cause true dialogue. I wonder if they believed there was anything worth fighting for. The sad thing was that here, in the hallowed halls of academia these professors, mostly men back then, were spewing their distorted beliefs on young, impressionable students, most of whom had never been exposed to any sort of real adversity. You could just sense the next generation of America-haters being born. It took great courage to offer a different point of view to someone who holds such power over your academic life which can affect your entire future. I had the feeling these proselytizing professors had actually convinced themselves these young students were mesmerized by their brilliance and insight. I think for the most part their young charges started out paying rapt attention in order to get good grades.

As time went by the more impressionable ones became brainwashed. But most of them would eventually go on to contribute to society by getting good jobs. They would live fulfilling lives, pay exorbitant taxes and have the government take their money and redistribute it to others. Some of them would be quite comfortable with this. Others would be stricken with guilt and become limousine liberals, enjoying both worlds of self-professed socialism while taking advantage of everything that capitalism has to offer. A certain number of them would go on to regurgitate the bile they were filled with and try to poison the minds of future generations.

Initially I would just sit there and try to concentrate on the courses. It became impossible to bear when they went from denigrating the war to denigrating the warrior. When their preaching went from their ignorant and perverted stance of rooting for the communists and condemning America to disrespecting those who had given up the privileges they enjoyed to help set other men free, I felt compelled to challenge that ignorance. I went home one day and asked my wife to sew an American flag (right-side-up) on the sleeve of my coat. I wanted to put all those professors and students on notice that their rants would not go unchallenged.

It wasn't just in the political science classes that this was happening. No matter what class I took, from English literature to psychology to meteorology, the odds were that part of the syllabus was sure to be that America was evil, and the war was criminal and immoral. From that day forward, I wore our flag on my jacket and when any lecture turned, as it invariably did, to Vietnam I would raise my hand, stand up and force a debate. I don't know if I changed anyone's mind or even caused them to think another way. I just knew I could not stand by and hear the groundless and clueless attacks made on my brothers.

It was hard to explain to the people in those classrooms that in war horrific things happen, the most horrific of all being the death of innocent civilians. But I would remind them that in World War II millions of civilians were killed. Whole cities were targeted for savage bombings. Cities like Dresden, Berlin, Nagasaki, Hiroshima and many others were literally destroyed. I tried to explain that we who had fought in wars wished that a gigantic magnet would descend from heaven and take away every gun, missile and bomb from the planet, but until that happened we had to be prepared and willing to fight those who truly would try to enslave us. We didn't even have to imagine what the alternative would be. We had only to look at history to see what appeasement to dictators like Hitler and Stalin brought to the world.

One professor smugly told me I was wrong. He said, "Haven't you heard about Ghandi?" I turned it back to him and asked, "How far do you think Ghandi would have gotten if he had tried to negotiate non-violently with Hitler or Stalin instead of Great Britain? I'm sure that six million Jews would have liked to *negotiate* with Adolph and fifty million dead Ukrainians would have just loved to sit down with 'Uncle Joe,' not to mention the tens of millions more these two rabid dogs eliminated." I must admit his comeback did leave me speechless. He looked me straight in the eyes and said, "Well, I'd rather be red than dead!" I had heard this sentiment before, along with the saying, "I'd rather live on my knees than die on my feet." The fact that this was coming from a teacher, someone who could mold young impressionable minds, made me sick to my stomach.

It was at that moment that I realized no logic could change these ideologues. Their beliefs had taken on a religious fervor that could not be moved. Like religion, it was a belief in things not seen. In all of history there had been no pure socialist or communist form of government that ever allowed anyone to prosper, anyone aside from a few elites at the top of the movement, yet still they believed these governments were the answer.

When they shouted they were the last bastion of free speech I asked why they censured and banned conservative speakers from the campus but demonstrated and protested to have such America-hating communists like Angela Davis speak? When I told them I had no problem with Ms. Davis speaking as long as the other side was also allowed to speak they would look at me with contempt failing to see any logic in my statement.

I had to assume they thought the only thing wrong with communism was that it hadn't been implemented correctly by the right people. I think they believed that they were the ones who could successfully implement the utopian life they envisioned. They were the enlightened ones who could make socialism/communism work. They were the elitists who would determine how to keep everyone the same under their brilliant leadership. Of course, a large amount of whatever resources might be realized would have to go to them, the leaders and planners so they could devote their time to use their superior brains to rule us.

In my mind they were ignorant, arrogant elitists and they were dangerous using their positions of trust and power to indoctrinate their charges and re-write history. By challenging almost everything being said I began to realize I was disrupting my classes. I had inherited my father's passion for learning but I knew I wouldn't be satisfied under these conditions.

I approached my professors and asked if I could pursue independent study courses. Under the independent study course path you could choose, with the approval of your professors, to study a subject on your own outside of the classroom. There was strict monitoring involved but you could either present your idea for approval or be given an assignment. There are a lot of grants given to universities and the departments and professors always needed people to assist in research. For some reason every professor I asked readily agreed to my request to study outside of his classroom.

For psychology, my major, I chose to pursue my interest of the workings of the minds of those who had undergone combat. I presented my outline and methods to my psych professor and he approved it. He told me to come to him if I needed anything. and to my surprise he seemed sincere when he said he would be interested in my findings.

It was about this time that my second daughter was born. Lisa was a beautiful calm child and a welcome addition to the family. I was still going to out-patient therapy at Lakeside and I scheduled my classes around it. Even though I was receiving a stipend for school and disability from the marines our money was very tight. My wife and I both preferred that she be home raising our girls. I was coming close to a crossroads and I would be making a choice that would close one door and open another.

The elevator doors on the psychiatric floor of the VA hospital opened and I walked down the long dull green painted hall. At the end of the hallway was a double steel door with two small windows about head high with no apparent door handles. On the right side of the door was a small box with a rounded mesh covering for you to speak into. Beneath the box was a red button. Beneath the button were the words "Call for service." I pressed the button and a voice said, "May I help you?" I stated my name and said I had an appointment with Doctor Hammer. Doctor Hammer was the Chief of Psychology at VA Lakeside. I called him the previous week and asked for an appointment. I explained my thesis and requested an interview. When he found out that I was a combat veteran he seemed eager to see me.

There was a loud buzz and the doors separated. A nurse met me on the other side of the door and led me to Doctor Hammer's office. He was a youthful looking man, affable with slightly graying hair. He had a firm handshake and I immediately liked him. He started the conversation by asking me about my background. I had the strange feeling he was interviewing me.

After I answered some of his questions I began the interview by having him state his name and position. I then began to ask a series of open ended questions, first asking for and receiving permission to record the interview. This was before the time that the term "post traumatic stress disorder" was ascribed to the condition of some Vietnam veterans. Doctor Hammer explained he noticed that most Vietnam veterans were making it through their combat experiences okay but were having some difficulty after coming home. He said they were noticing that the psychiatric wards were becoming more and more crowded one, two and three years after the men had returned home. He posited that he believed a big problem was the basic isolation experienced by the troops. He explained that unlike other wars where men were shipped off to combat with the same men they trained with, the men in Vietnam were sent as line replacements for those killed or wounded to units as needed. That meant they went overseas by themselves.

They were sent on commercial airliners that had been contracted by the government. It would take a while to assimilate into the unit. It was hard to fit in because no one wanted to invest too much energy into establishing an emotional attachment to someone who may be quickly wounded or killed. Once a certain amount of time passed and you were accepted into the group the bonds that were formed were unbreakable. At the end of your tour or if you were disabled by a wound you would return home by yourself.

In World War II you would return with the same unit you trained and fought with on a long boat trip home. You were placed in a camp where you would be reassigned or discharged. This gave you time to decompress. The cohesiveness and support nurtured by such a structure went a long way in the healing process. That's not to say that men were not affected. Just watch when some of the World War II veterans are interviewed today about their war experiences. You'll see that even after all these years many of them break down with uncontrollable emotions. When you understand these emotions are still displayed in a generation that basically had the support of the nation, was called the "Greatest Generation", and came home to the cheers, gratitude and admiration of their fellow countrymen you can start to understand the types of feelings the Vietnam veterans were having.

Doctor Hammer went on to say that he was studying these effects as the possible reasons that men were seeking help after being home for some time. Into this theory of isolation was the knowledge of what was happening to the returning servicemen. I added that war is war, no matter if it was the Revolutionary War, The Civil War, World Wars I or II, Korea or Vietnam. It didn't matter how sophisticated the weapons were. The experiences, sacrifices and hardships of the individual combat soldier were universal. Vietnam was proving that the peripheral issues like politics, class warfare, guilt and the denigration of America's traditional values by the elites could be just as lethal or more so than an enemy bullet.

At the end of the interview I thanked Doctor Hammer for his time and graciousness. To my surprise he asked me what my plans were. I told him that at this time I was hoping to finish school and ultimately enter business. He said that a major in psychology was an interesting choice in the pursuit of a business career. He said it was interesting but completely understandable. If you understood the mind you could understand what motivates people to make the decisions they make..

He then said something that I would never have anticipated. He asked me that before I made up my mind would I consider an alternative. He asked me if I would consider staying in the psychology field and volunteer to work for him while I was going through school. He said that if I liked it I could possibly work with him after I got my degree. He said that my being a combat veteran as well as a disabled one would be an advantage in assisting him in his studies. I thanked him and told him I would think about it and get back to him.

I handed in my course work and received an "A" for the course. As a matter of fact for that semester I made the dean's list. I ultimately made up my mind regarding Doctor Hammer's offer. I thought it would be a tremendous opportunity for someone to be involved in such important work. However, to become involved would mean to continue in an environment that I had no respect for. In addition with two children a wife and already being years behind my contemporaries in the race for jobs and careers I decided to leave the university and enter real life.

I was about to go through a new door. I wasn't quite sure what was on the other side but I knew I had to do it, though I felt some trepidation. When I was in hospitals I was surrounded by men with disabilities worse than mine and felt that my wound was not an issue. I was now about to enter and compete in a world where most people had all their body parts functioning as they should. I was also not sure of how my experience in Vietnam would be received. I had heard from fellow veterans that some of them were leaving their service to their country off their resume due to some of the reactions they had initially received from prospective employers. The elite of the media, newspapers, television and Hollywood thought it was their duty to portray Vietnam Veterans as drug crazed losers who committed horrendous crimes in their articles, dramas and films. Of course in their zeal to denigrate those who viewed the world differently from them they omitted the patriotism, bravery and self-sacrifice of the vast majority of those who served for selfless reasons. They refused to tell the story of how more drugs were being consumed on college campuses and in the neighborhoods than what was being consumed on the battlefields of Vietnam.

One of the lies I really enjoyed was that we joined the service for the money. When I joined the marines the starting salary was ninety dollars per month. Even later with overseas pay and combat pay I don't think my income reached four hundred dollars per month.

As I reflected on the recent past, Vietnam, hospitals, rehabilitation and school I was sure of one thing. I felt an enormous pride in what I had done. I had overcome adversity and was still left with an unswerving love of my country and belief in what it stood for. I was somewhat shaky on how my disability would affect my career possibilities but I felt that although physical labor requiring two hands was most probably out, I believed I could accomplish success once I recognized my path.

One thing that Doctor Hammer had discussed was the concept of the Vietnam veteran having a solitary experience. That's not to say the experiences of combat were so dissimilar. On the contrary much of the experiences of combat were universal. His solitary theory was that the Vietnam veteran pretty much went through this life altering experience, alone.

Where am I going?
How do I get there?
What should I bring along?

Are people kind there?
Is peace of mind there?
Will I finally belong?

Some poets say that,
There'll come a day that,
I'll find a place for me.

Why aren't I there yet?
Why can't I share yet?
Why can't my heart be free?

'Cause you know that
Ships sail their courses
And heroes ride horses,
They know where they belong.

But I travel in circles
Quickly to nowhere
Singing my unfinished song.

Lyrics to "Unfinished Song"
by
Charles S. Lofrano

CHAPTER SEVEN

Assimilation

South Side of Chicago/
Mokena, Illinois

With my family growing, I now had two daughters, Deana Christine and Lisa Marie, I needed to get my life back together. As a result I left the unreal world of academia and started looking for a job. Not being able to use my arm greatly diminished the possibility of seeking physical employment. I had taken a series of aptitude tests at the VA hospital while receiving rehab. The results showed I could do well as a teacher or in marketing /sales. My experiences with some of the professors at The University of Illinois at Chicago Circle Campus were enough to convince me that the academic community was not for me.

Over my life I have been exposed to many different types of people and institutions, i.e.: church, the marines, many hospital and doctor groups, small businesses, corporate America, charity organizations, political groups, the music industry, and veterans organizations. Of these I found the academic community to be the most demagogic, self-righteous, closed-minded, arrogant and power obsessed institution of them all. So as I ruled out the teaching profession and any meaningful job requiring the use of two arms, in my mind the only option left was in marketing/sales. Unfortunately as I looked through the want ads I found that most sales positions that offered decent pay and good benefits with a path toward advancement required experience. My DD214 (Discharge Document) from the Marine Corps read as follows: "MOS (Military Occupational Specialty), 0331 M60 Machine Gunner, related civilian occupation, 'Weapons. ". So, unless I wanted to get a job as a hit man for organized crime, I was pretty much out of luck.

Meanwhile my bills kept piling up. We found a two-bedroom apartment on Edbrooke Street on the south side and with car payments, baby food, clothes and utilities, etc. things were getting tight. But I never felt like a victim or that these conditions would be permanent. Many of us who had spent time in hell came away with a basic philosophy. Whenever things in life seemed to overwhelm us we would have a tendency to shrug our shoulders and say, "What more can you do to me, send me to Vietnam?" When that sentiment was invoked it usually brought about a sense of perspective. How hard were the transient disappointments in life compared to the savagery and devastation of combat? Life is hard for everyone. It's those who can overcome hardships and keep on trying who will find themselves winners in the end.

It is true that some of us did not assimilate well back in the world but the fact remains that the overwhelming majority of Vietnam veterans eventually went on to live productive and fulfilling lives. Unfortunately for us, those who chose not to go were the ones who defined us as drug users and losers. Many of them became professors journalists, politicians and opinion makers.

This time for me was an intense period of adjustment. These were the times when I, and I am sure many others, were going through a barrage of conflicting emotions. Relief at making it home, guilt for leaving our brothers dead or still fighting when we left and a clouded vision of what lay ahead of us. There was also a fear of those who were permanently disabled if they would be able to compete in this changing world.

My sense of conflict resolution was also becoming confused Before the war I was willing to use physical force to resolve differences that might occur pretty much as a display of childish bravado in order to prove myself. During the war it became clear to me where the use of physical force could lead. One day soon after I came home I was attempting to parallel park in front of my fathers house. I hadn't noticed that a car had come speeding up behind me. It must have either started at the end of the block or turned from a side street. Regardless, when I stopped to begin my back up to park I heard a loud screech as the car behind me came to a sudden stop and missed my rear bumper by mere inches. After a short time, the car pulled around and stopped on my left side. I noticed there were two young men in the front. They stared at me for a short time. As I stared at them I sensed that there was a combination of fear and anger in their countenance. Fear at the realization that they just missed an accident and anger at the object of their fear.

I still wore the cast I was given in Japan and it was visible as I rested it on the door with the window down. The driver leaned forward to stare at me around the passenger to his right. He cursed me and threatened to "break my other arm." My first reaction was to get out of my car and confront him but instead I heard myself tell him to just move on and slow down in the neighborhood. He stared at me a short time more and then sped off. That incident bothered me for a long time afterward. At first I thought I had been a coward for not jumping out of the car and confronting the driver. Later I came to realize that I was now at a place where I did not want to engage in violence, because if I was ever forced into it I would not stop until my adversary was unable to come back at me.

I had killed men so I knew what I was capable of. This realization further alienated me from the rest of society and contributed to my feelings of isolation. Two other incidents among others stood out. On the first fourth of July after I got home I was driving down the street with Pam. Everything was going along fine until a string of firecrackers blew off to the side of my car. Without any conscious thought I immediately slammed on my brakes, grabbed Pam by the shoulders and dove to the floor of the car. My defense mechanisms kicked in to what seemed like gunshots and I reacted automatically to a threatening situation. To this day I still experience a slight start to the sound of fireworks no matter how many times I remind myself that it is not gunfire.

Another occurrence really bothered me and caused me deep concern. Pam loves to laugh and as a result she is prone to play practical jokes. One night after I had been home for a while, my mother sent me to drop off something at my aunt's home. She lived on the top floor of a three flat on west 111th Street. I asked Pam to wait in the car and I entered the building. As I entered I noticed there was no elevator and the first floor vestibule was dark. I found a chain hanging down from a light bulb but when I pulled it nothing happened. I remembered thinking that I would warn my elderly aunt and tell her to inform her landlord. I climbed the three flights, dropped off my mother's items, warned my aunt of the darkness in her hallway and descended the stairwell.

Due to the darkness my instincts were working overtime. As in the black night of the jungle, sight lost importance. It was replaced by a highly enhanced sense of smell and hearing. In addition, an unexplainable awareness overtakes you. It's like having your nerves on the outside of your body. As I got closer to the ground floor those outside nerves were tingling. My mind became calm, focused and pulsated energy outward like radar. I felt my body going into combat mode ready for anything. All of a sudden a body came out of the darkness. I turned and had my hand around the person's neck and was staring directly into their face angrily for a split second before I realized that it was Pam. She had thought it would be funny to scare me. Needless to say we were both frightened. I think Pam and I realized that I was definitely not the same person I had been before I left.

In spite of these conflicting emotions I still believed that if you want to change and improve your life you have to get off your ass and do something. The journey will be perilous and daunting and, unless your name is Kennedy or Rockefeller and you have wealth handed to you through no exertions of your own, the chances are good that you will experience failures and roadblocks. You will have to overcome or go around the obstacles presented to you to reach your goal. I didn't realize it at the time but I would draw on my experiences in Vietnam, including my survival instincts, so well honed there to overcome adversities created by others as well as those created by me.

From now on my decisions and outlook would be seen through the prism of Vietnam. The war was over for me but I knew it would never go away. I instinctively knew it was the same with veterans from all wars. For most of us it would not permanently paralyze our actions or impede our advancement. It would always be there just below the surface, not dictating our lives but acting as a consultant to how we would live our lives and what would be important and have value.

A friend of mine turned me on to my first job after I got home. He worked for a major national retail and catalogue store that was headquartered in Chicago. A position became available in the display and store planning department, which coordinated all the in-store signage from design to content and standardized the look for all the stores throughout the nation. It was an entry-level position and the starting salary was low but there were benefits and a path toward advancement. It was a way to gain experience as well as starting my resume with the name of a large, well-known, major corporation. Of course, the best part about it was an opportunity to work.

Since it was an entry-level position no direct experience was required. I interviewed with the head of the department and found out I wouldn't be starting in the creative area. I would be starting in the more basic aspects of collecting the ideas already created in photos and print copy that were assembled on boards and I would work with various printers and screen printers to create in-store advertising and the instructions on how and where to place the signage that would be distributed to the chain.

In the interview I glossed over my military record and I must have made a good impression because I was offered the position that day. I was eager to get into the working world. I felt my life had been put on hold and I wanted desperately to start this new adventure. I attacked each new skill I was taught like I was assaulting a hill. I sized up the situation, mentally calculated the importance of the mission, focused all my attention and attacked.

After about a year a pattern was starting to set in. I was doing well on the job and although I had received some raises and a promotion, I was getting restless. It came to a head on my second performance review. My boss was a likeable man and I respected him but when he gave me his assessment I felt compelled to leave. He told me I was doing a good job and if I continued to do so I would most likely , eventually get his job when he retired. The uncontrollable thought that instantly leapt to my mind was, "Why would I want your job?" I felt bad when I looked at him and saw the expression on his face. He seemed disappointed and confused when my countenance did not match his anticipation. I meant no disrespect to him or his position. It was just that after my life and death experiences, his offer left me empty.

It was soon after this incident that I left the company. One of my co-workers was leaving for a top position with one of our suppliers and asked me to come with him. The next few years were pretty much like that. Just as I began to feel comfortable and competent and a closeness to my co-workers, I started looking for a way out. It was almost as if I was still living under the rules of Vietnam warfare. The warnings that had been drummed into my psyche were surfacing unbidden to my consciousness. "Don't make friends, it's too dangerous. Don't hope. Don't become attached, it can all be gone in an instant!"

Another problem was that I would become bored very quickly. Still another was that I realized I was chasing money and not a career. Instinctively I knew I belonged in sales but my attention was always being diverted by the need to immediately increase my income by starting a new job that would offer me more money. I didn't realize that this was a recipe for failure. Intellectually I knew that the small salary increases would not compensate for the loss of income caused by not staying at a job long enough to become valuable to an employer.

Emotionally, in addition to the issues of attachment, I just could not follow the conformity and rules it took to fit in and advance in an organization. I needed to be in a profession where I could control my income and succeed based on my skills and abilities. I needed the freedom and opportunity to do battle, take the hill and leave others to police the area and occupy the ground while I went to take the next hill. I needed to be in sales.

Once again I hit the want ads and once again I felt blocked by the requirement of the need for experience. The money situation was getting tighter. My brilliant strategy of changing jobs was not working and I was not building any kind of future. It was becoming a vicious circle. I would get excited by a new job, become bored and disillusioned and then ultimately quit or get fired. This would be followed by sadness, self-loathing, guilt and great bouts of depression that would leave me immobilized.

It was during this time that I experienced another miracle. At the age of eleven I started playing the tenor saxophone. I wasn't great but I was good enough to play in a small band at local dances and weddings. I never seriously thought of making music a career but I enjoyed playing immensely. After I was wounded it became apparent I could no longer play the sax. In a fit of anger and self-pity I called my old sax teacher and asked him if he knew of anyone who would want to buy my sax, a Mark VI Selmer. It was considered a Cadillac in the world of musical instruments. It cost six hundred dollars some eleven years previously and was the type of instrument that if kept in good condition could not only hold its value but had a possibility of increasing in value.

My teacher called back and said so far he had only one person interested but although he really wanted the horn he was currently out of work and only could afford fifty dollars. He said he was sorry and he would keep on trying. I found myself telling him to go ahead and sell it. I think the fact that the saxophone was a constant reminder of how my life had been altered caused me to want to get rid of it.

Arrangements were made for my teacher to pick up my sax and give me the fifty dollars. I didn't want to know the name of the buyer. After the transaction I put it out of my mind. It was another emotional hit that I attempted to bury deep inside. I never thought of it again until that morning when it seemed like my entire world was coming apart. I had been trying to balance the bills, paying those that definitely had to be paid and making partial payments on those that could be put off. On that apocalyptic morning I was faced with a warning from my landlord and a final disconnect notice on the electric bill. It wasn't much money but it was more than I had. I sat down not knowing what to do. I felt like a miserable failure who had let his family down.

I was ashamed to tell my wife. I called my creditors to ask for more time and was refused. Then, all of a sudden I became calm. It was like combat. I would enter a fight with fear and anxiety. At some point I would just let go and become willing to accept whatever the outcome. I've come to realize that this is the essence of prayer. You can use all your talents, skill and experience to overcome what you could. When the situation becomes overwhelming and beyond our control the only thing we can do is "Let go and let God". That morning I let go and put my trust in God. Still not knowing what I was going to do, I walked downstairs from our third floor apartment to get my mail. My heart sunk lower as the first few pieces of mail were more bills.

Suddenly, my interest was peaked by a hand-addressed envelope with a name under the sender's address I did not recognize. My thought was that it was probably from an attorney looking for payment for one of their clients. I walked slowly upstairs into my apartment and sat down at the kitchen table. I put the obvious items aside to open later. I drew the handwritten letter from the bills and placed it by itself on the table in front of me. Before I opened it I got up and poured myself a cup of coffee, came back to the table and sat down.

I lit a cigarette and opened the letter. As I began the letter I couldn't believe what I was reading. It was the closest I had felt to God since that day in Vietnam in 1968 when a naval doctor just happened to be passing by to hear my protestations after being told my arm was to be amputated. The letter was from the man who bought my saxophone about seven months prior. He explained that he knew he had not paid enough for the horn at the time. He said he was sorry but at the time he just couldn't afford more. He said he always felt bad about it but it was all he could do. Up to that point I thought this was a gracious thank you from a grateful person and my spirit was starting to rise. I was not, however, prepared for what I read next.

He went on to say that since he bought my saxophone his fortune had started to change. He got an audition with the band that played on *Bozo's Circus*, a local WGN TV show, and had gotten the job. He credited his good fortune with the fact that his Selmer Mark IV saxophone with its gold plating, French scrolling and deep, rich melodious tone gave him the confidence to play better than he had ever played in his life. As I read further, a chill covered my body and my eyes filled with tears. He went on to say that due to this turn of events his life and financial status had changed drastically and he hoped I would accept the check he had sent me with the letter. I looked inside the envelope and there, wrapped inside a folded piece of paper, was a check. It wasn't a huge amount but it was more than I needed to pay the immediate bills including the rent.

    This incident gave me new hope. By the end of the week I had already started working on finding a new job. Intuitively I knew my calling was sales. The best shot I felt I had to make some money, learn the basics and get some training, was in the car business. The reason I chose the car business was that many dealers at that time were offering sales jobs with no sales experience for commission only. Some offered a draw for a limited period of time. A draw was basically a loan by the dealer in lieu of salary. It would offer the salesman some money so that he would have an income while he learned the business. The down side of a draw was that it had to be paid back from earned commission. This seems a bit harsh but if you think about it, it does make sense for both parties. For the dealer it allows him to offer a position to someone who would have to prove they could do the job. The draw was usually for three months and the most they would risk would be a small amount of money. If the employee worked out the dealer would feel more confident to offer a salary and the use of a new car to drive as a demo. For the employee it was a way to enter the world of sales and gain experience. It was a place for them to learn that although from the outside sales looked easy, if they were smart and observant they would soon learn that it was hard work and that ten percent of all salesmen earned ninety percent of the money.

If you were suited for the profession three months was just about the right amount of time to identify the basics. It took longer to become proficient but in those first three months you could begin to learn the importance of identifying buyers, uncovering their buying criteria and ability to afford their choice by asking a series of questions. You could learn to negotiate and, most important, how to close a deal. You could learn how to keep your customer happy and satisfied so they would remain your customer and recommend you to their friends and family. Car salespeople have gotten a bad name over the years because again, only ten percent of salespeople in any industry are true professionals. The other ninety percent don't have a clue.

I sold cars for the next few years. I was relatively successful but I knew I wanted to move on in the sales profession. I would ultimately have a very successful sales career working in both start-up companies and multi-billion dollar corporations earning six figure incomes. But I will always attribute my success to the basics I learned at that Pontiac dealership on 89th & Ashland on Chicago's south side.

When I decided to make the move from consumer sales to business sales I felt pretty confident. I was also starting to successfully keep Vietnam and the aftermath of it buried deep inside of me, or so I believed. Although my working life was starting to click my personal life was still strained. I still felt isolated. I would rarely go out of my apartment except to go to work. I only wanted to be around the small number of people I felt safe with; my wife, my two beautiful daughters and my sisters. I also had two friends outside this family ring that I felt comfortable with.

Paul was a friend from the old neighborhood on the south side. We joined the marines at the same time and were in ITR together. We were sent to Vietnam at the same time and both of us had been wounded. He became godfather to one of my daughters and I became godfather to one of his daughters. We eventually lived across the street from each other and spent a great deal of time crossing that street to play cards together with our wives. Paul entered law enforcement and was voted into the position of sheriff of the second largest county in Illinois for two consecutive terms by double-digit margins and I am sure that Paul's service to others is not over yet. Paul is the type of man that if you were to ask for a hand he'd give you his whole arm.

When Paul came to see me after he got home from Vietnam, my tour had been cut short due to my disabling wound while he served his full tour, it was the first time I talked in depth about my experiences since my hospital days. As Paul and I shared our war stories I hadn't noticed that my wife was standing in the kitchen overhearing what we were saying. Not knowing Pam was listening we had been very graphic about what we had seen. At one point Paul reached in his pocket and started to pull out a hand-gun. He was working for a security company at the time and wanted to show me the new .38 he had been issued. The sight of the gun together with the horror of the stories Pam had heard were too much for her. She let out a shriek and ran from the apartment. I realized what had happened and ran after her. I apologized and explained why Paul had drawn the gun. This incident was further proof to me that even those closest to us would never fully understand us nor should they be expected to. After that I would only talk in depth about Vietnam to other veterans except for Dennis.

As I previously mentioned, Dennis DeYoung was one of the founding members of the successful rock group Styx. The other two founding members were my first cousins, John and Chuck Panozzo. I had been very close to them. We saw each other constantly at our parents and grandparents houses and at family functions and our families went on vacations together. Although John and Chuck were twins and a year older, we had gone to the same grammar school and the same high school. They both stood up for my wedding and I was a pallbearer at John's funeral. It was through them at about the age of thirteen that I met Dennis.

Dennis was not only one of the few people outside the veterans' community I could talk to, he also embodied all the things I believed in regarding the promise of America. He rose from a modest working class background to create one of the great rock 'n' roll bands of the seventies selling multi-platinum and gold albums and touching the lives of countless millions by the songs he wrote. We became very close friends and I was fortunate to be able to write a few of their early songs. As of this writing we have been married to two beautiful sisters for over thirty-seven years.

Seeing the depth of Dennis's character over time I became more and more comfortable in discussing Vietnam with him. I never felt that he judged me or that he would think any less of me. Later on he would come to the aid of the veteran community in a huge way for no money and not much recognition.

I finally came to the conclusion that the future for me was in the information technology industry. It wasn't called that back then but you didn't have to be a guru to know where things were going. This was before the dawn of the PC revolution when companies were still struggling to find ways to capture and manage great amounts of information. Mainframe computers were the order of the day. They were huge, very expensive and not too efficient for small to midsize companies. They were a tremendous improvement over old labor intensive methods but carried their own liabilities.

Highly trained and highly paid programmers were needed to run them. All processing was done on the mainframe and the end user was connected by a terminal. No matter how fast the mainframe, a priority of tasks had to be established. Who would get their jobs done first? Would it be accounts payable, accounts receivable, administration, sales, marketing, R&D? The data processing departments became kingdoms within companies. Since the technology and language associated with the mainframe culture was so obscure most people other than engineers and programmers had no idea what was going on. They only knew that raw data was given to these mystical beings and somehow meaningful reports were returned to them.

There was competition between departments to get their jobs scheduled first. Sometimes even the presidents of corporations were at the mercy of these wizards. Since the bosses didn't understand how these miracles were performed, they had to rely on the consul of the data processing managers. The mainframes were great at crunching billions of bytes of data in an application, but not so good at handling dozens of different applications at the same time. It wasn't until PCs were fully developed with servers, networks and compatible user-friendly software (thank you

IBM, Compaq, Novell, Cisco Systems and Microsoft) that small to midsize businesses could compete, grow and employ millions of people to drive our economy to dizzying new heights. For the first time a worker without a programming or engineering degree could pull down an application from a server over a high-speed network and work on the data at their own workstation, manipulate the data and do so on their own schedule.

I experienced this evolution/revolution after I entered the field but I did have a strong sense that the efficient management and storage of data was the next phase after the Industrial Revolution that had changed the commerce of this country from agriculture to manufacturing and automation. A whole new world was opening up and a new breed of Americans were being summoned to make the transition. Men and women of entrepreneurial spirit with courage and drive entered the field looking for excitement and a pathway to money and success unencumbered by the old rules. Men like Bill Gates, who actually dropped out of college, would become billionaires due to their vision and creativity rather than as a result of how many degrees they had. It also gave people like me a level field entering this new uncharted field. We could be judged for what we did. A degree would get you in the door easier but you had to adapt and overcome in order to be successful in this new universe. Adapt and overcome. Now that was something I had experience in.

So, in the mid-seventies I decided to go into the information industry. This was about ten years before the PCs went from personal home use to becoming an essential business tool. At that time I cleaned up pretty good and generally made a good impression, and my limited experience working for a national corporation and experience in selling cars gave me the confidence needed to give a good interview. I bought a tailored suit with the left sleeve shortened an inch more than the right one and it became hard to notice that there was something wrong with my arm.

I called for and got an interview with a multi-billion dollar, multi-national corporation. They had three divisions. There was a data processing division that handled mainframe computers, a general systems division which covered smaller computers and an office products division that sold products like electric typewriters, copiers, dictating equipment and the emerging technology of self-supporting memory typewriters and word processors. I knew there was no way I qualified for DP or GSD but I felt I could handle the line of the office products division. A large and mid-range computer was a very expensive purchase. It required the customer to make changes in how he did business. As a result the decision making process was much longer and much more involved. In addition, the company I was interviewing with had the corner on the large to mid-range computer market so the success of the sale was pretty much determined by the product and the company. The salesmen of these divisions had to be more account managers and experts in computer knowledge.

The OPD salesmen had to be more like gunfighters. Although the company's name was well known, the office products field was saturated. The average sales of a large to mid-range computer with software and maintenance could be in the millions while a sale in the office products marketplace could be in the hundreds. The OPD salesman had to go out and make things happen everyday. This type of action appealed to me greatly. Once again on my application and in my interview I glossed over my military experience. I also made no mention of my disability. This was in the days when there was no strong "Americans with Disabilities Act", nor were there the strict privacy laws that exist today. Back then, when applying for a sales position, your employer could ask such questions as, "Are you married? Do you have any children? Do you own your own home? What kind of car do you drive?" These questions were asked to determine how eager you would be and how hard you would work to make money for yourself and your company.

Before I started earning six figures I once lost out on a job because the manager asked me if I had ever made over a hundred thousand dollars. When I answered that I had not yet achieved that amount he said he was sorry but if I wasn't used to making that kind of money they had no need for me.

The interview for the OP division went well and I was told they would check my resume and call me back with their decision. A few days later I got a call from the branch manager saying he wanted me to come in. I arrived at his office and was directed to take a seat in front of his desk. He told me he was impressed with me but he had a concern. He said his last few hires had been MBAs. He stopped, stared at me and asked me how I felt about that. I became calm as I stared back at him. With no hesitation I let go mentally and heard myself say, " Do you want an MBA or someone who can sell?" As soon as I said it I knew it was what he wanted to hear. I had just given him the reason he was looking for to hire me.

He buzzed for his assistant to call in the man who was to be my sales manager. The man who walked through the door looked like the cover of GQ Magazine. He had clear, piercing blue eyes and short cropped brown hair. He wore a standard white starched button down shirt, red tie and immaculately tailored blue pin-striped suit with matching vest. I found out later that the women in the office called him "Mr. Eight by Ten." The branch manager introduced us and asked me to wait outside his office while they talked. After a while the sales manager came out and asked me to follow him to his office. He explained the basic duties of the position and mentioned that I would have to go to Dallas for two weeks of training. He asked me why I wanted the job and what made me think I could be successful. I told him I wanted the opportunity to work for such an esteemed corporation. I also told him I was eager to achieve my financial goals and I believed I could do that by helping him and the corporation achieve theirs. I told him I was confident I could accomplish that task. He smiled, shook my hand and welcomed me. He said they originally were concerned that I did not have an MBA, but the fact that I had been successful in a commission-only sales position and I had some songs published proved that I had drive and creativity.

I felt elated that I had been accepted by this high profile, multi-billion dollar corporation. I also felt validated. Perhaps the disparaging things being said about me and my fellow veterans weren't true. Maybe we weren't the bottom rung of society after all. I was told to see the AA (administrative assistant) and have her make an appointment for a physical and based on the outcome I could start in two weeks and join the class that was scheduled for the next training session in Dallas.

Suddenly I panicked! I desperately hoped that my outward countenance didn't betray the crushing feeling I had inside. They were going to find out about my arm! All around me I saw the image that they wanted to portray: bright, attractive young men and women with all their parts working. Although I was in my twenties I still felt like a forty-year-old man after the experiences I had been through. I was sure that after the physical they would either flat out rescind their offer because I didn't fit in or rescind the offer because I had not told them of my disability. I must have been a better salesman than I thought because as I looked in the eyes of my potential manager I could see no detection of the fear and anxiety I was feeling inside.

I shook his hand, thanked him and walked over to the AA's desk. She was businesslike and efficient as she scheduled the physical for the next week. She said the results should be back by the Wednesday before the Monday that I would start working. I drove home trying to convince myself that everything was going to be okay. They liked me. I had gotten an offer on the second interview. Besides, even if they rejected me it wasn't like they were going to send me to Vietnam.

That last thought was not too comforting when Wednesday came around and I received no call. Nor was it anymore reassuring when Thursday rolled around and still no call came. I drove my wife crazy by agonizing endlessly over the silence of the telephone. I was building up my courage that Friday to contact them when I finally got a call from the branch manager. He asked me if I could come in on Monday an hour before the regular starting time to meet with him and his two sales managers. I asked him if there were any problems and if I would be starting work after that. I was hoping this was some sort of orientation session before I began work. All he said was that it was important.

Shit, that was it! I thought, "Nice try, Lofrano, you almost got there." Maybe I was that piece of crap loser all those college kids, professors, journalists and Hollywood elites were saying I was. After all, they were the enlightened ones on the planet weren't they? Maybe the things I'd done disqualified me for civilized living. Why should I go down there just to be humiliated? Then I thought, "No, fuck them!" If they were going to destroy me they would have to do it to my face. Once again I used a lesson learned in Vietnam. "Charge the ambush! If you just lay there, you will die."

That Monday, after a terrible, sleepless weekend, I arrived early for my appointment and was led to the branch manager's office. He was not behind his desk but instead was seated at a large, heavy looking round table. On either side of him were the two sales managers of the office. He motioned for me to take a seat. The three of them looked at me pleasantly enough but I was operating on my survival instincts and I sensed the men were tense. The sales managers looked to be a few years older than me but the branch manager was probably about thirty years older. To me this meant that he was from the old school. One of the gunfighters who helped build the reputation of the corporation. One of those who helped put it on the map. I found myself not only desperately wanting the job but also wanting to get his respect.

He began by telling me they reviewed the report of my physical. He wondered why I had not mentioned my disability in my interview. I said I didn't mention it because I didn't think it was relevant. He replied that in the office products division there were times when I would have to lift and install heavy equipment like electronic and memory typewriters. He asked me the same question he had asked me when he told me about their MBA preference. "How do you feel about that?" Once again I let go and became calm. The first thought that came to me was, "How do those small, slim women I see in your office handle it?

My battle sense kicked in and I immediately recognized that this would not be an appropriate response so I used a variation on the answer I had given when asked about the MBA issue. I looked into the eyes of each of them one at a time. I stood up, smiled, put both my hands on the rim of the heavy round table and once again answered a question with a question. "Gentlemen, if I lift this table, can I have this job?" There was an instant of wide-eyed surprise followed by nervous laughter. They looked at each other, nodding, and then each of the sales managers extended a hand and welcomed me to the corporation. The old gunfighter shook my hand last and said, "Great close."

The training I received in Dallas was intense. It was geared towards product knowledge(OPD sold a variety of items), interviewing prospective customers, phone techniques, establishing buying criteria and closing the deal. From a developed and tested process you were to determine which of your products could benefit the client, present the solution, demonstrate the product to their need to ultimately consummate the deal and make money change hands. They brought in successful salesmen from all over the country to instruct us and to play the role of customers on whom you could practice and be judged on what you were learning.

On the last day of training we were tested and graded on what we had learned. We were lined up in a hall that had doors on each side. We were to enter an office and assume we had already established the right for an appointment with a perspective client. Seated behind a desk was one of the superstar" salesmen from the field role playing as a client. In an allotted period of time we were to find out what the client needed, gain his agreement that we had in fact uncovered those needs and demonstrate the product tailored to solve those needs. The salesman would be sitting there answering and asking questions with an evaluation sheet to make sure we hit all the right buttons.

While I waited for my turn I felt as though I were back in boot camp where all our training culminated in the final physical fitness test. If we failed the final test we were required to go back to the beginning of training with a new training regiment and start all over again while the other members of our unit went on to graduate. I didn't think we would be set back or lose our jobs if we didn't do well but I had a strong sense that in this corporation every success or failure would be noted.

I was more than pleased with the outcome of my test. After I went through all the techniques and did a demo and close, the salesman gave me a copy of his evaluation sheet. There was a scale of one to five next to each of the techniques to indicate how we had done in each category, i.e. questioning, listening, demo, trial close, close, etc. He had given me a five in each category and written "Chuck presented the best damned demo in Dallas." I was so relieved and happy that I didn't mind not getting the award for best student of the class. No one had told me that one of the criteria was being helpful to other students. Throughout the class I had maintained my normal modus operandi and stayed pretty much to myself.

I believe this was the greatest, most professional and most meaningful sales training I ever attended, and I have attended many of them. Even when I became a sales training manager for other companies and taught classes myself, I tried to emulate the exceptional and extremely successful techniques I was fortunate to have received in Dallas. Between this and my Marine Corps training, I felt ready to take on the world.

As time went on the culture changed again. Instead of building companies with superior products, outstanding customer service and hard-working, dedicated personnel, the order of the day became mergers and corporate takeovers. Why try to compete for market share when you could just buy up your competition? The days of the bean counters had arrived pushing out those creative, innovative visionaries that made America the envy of the rest of the world. It took them a while but they were able to change the landscape when the American automobile business went from number one in the world to an also ran. We were now looking forward to the next three months as opposed to the next three years; quarterly, not yearly, profits were the goal. The large corporations moved away from the gunfighter salesmen. They were too costly and they felt they weren't needed with the advent of new account management software and they were probably right. The large corporations marketed themselves on their size and their financial picture measured in a large way by the expanding global marketplace.

The hardcore sales training days were being replaced with the pitiful concepts of "Team Building," touchy-feely games being passed off as meaningful learning experiences. Instead of learning your product line and perfecting your skills in simulated real life business situations you were subjected to idiotic exercises. One such exercise was to team up two people. One of these people was blindfolded and given a golf club, then the other person directed him on how to hit the ball and adjust for more precision. There were other childish games liker scavenger hunts, passing through a maze of string, making up songs with input from all members of your team, etc. I always felt these to be a complete waste of precious selling time and resources. The only ones I could conceive of benefiting from those frivolities were the companies that convinced somebody that these bogus exercises had meaning. Perhaps for administrative people or middle managers or account managers these games could foster an atmosphere of camaraderie. But for the salesman, the gunfighter, the pioneer who had to go out, make something happen and cause money to change hands, this was an insult.

By definition the gunfighter had to think outside the box. He had to be sharp, creative and not have to go back to check with a committee on what he should do. If he were good enough, and the true gunfighters definitely were, they would know not to oversell their company's abilities. They would know not to over promise. The true professional knew that all he had was his time and integrity. The customer could always buy a similar product from anywhere, so it did no good to make one sale to a company and then not follow through with that client. One reason was you probably would never sell to that person again. Another was that the longer you serviced your client well , the more you would find your reputation would proceed you, especially if you stayed in the same industry.

A successful sales campaign was like a military operation. Marketing and advertising were like air strikes and artillery used to soften the beach. The account managers were the occupation troops that controlled the objective once it was taken. But it was the infantry, the salesman, who charged the hill, took the fire and won the battle yard by bloody yard.

Anonymous:

"A couple of years ago someone asked me if I still thought about Vietnam. I nearly laughed in their face. How do you stop thinking about it? Every day for the last twenty-four years, I wake up with it and go to bed with it, but this is what I said, 'Yea, I think about it. I can't quit thinking about it. I never will. But, I've learned to live with it. I'm comfortable with the memories. I've learned to stop trying to forget and learned instead to embrace it. It just doesn't scare me anymore.'

A psychiatrist once told me that not being affected by the experience over there would be abnormal. When he told me that, it was like he'd just given me a pardon. It was as if he said, 'Go ahead and feel something about the place. It ain't going nowhere. You're gonna wear it for the rest of your life. Might as well get to know it.'

A lot of my 'brothers' haven't been so lucky. For them the memories are too painful, their sense of loss too great. My sister told me of a friend she has whose husband was in the Nam. She asks this guy when he was there. Here's what he said, 'Just last night.' It took my sister a while to figure out what he was talking about. JUST LAST NIGHT. Yea, I was in the Nam. When? JUST LAST NIGHT. During sex with my wife. And on my way to work this morning. Over my lunch hour. Yea, I was there.

My sister says I'm not the same brother that went to Vietnam. My wife says I won't let people get close to me, not even her. They are probably both right.

Ask a vet about making friends in Nam. It was risky. Why? Because we were in the business of death, and death was with us all the time. It wasn't the death of 'If I die before I wake.' This was the real thing. The kind where boys scream for their mothers. The kind that lingers in your mind and becomes more real each time you cheat it. You don't want to make a lot of friends when the possibility of dying is that real, that close. When you do, friends become a liability.

A guy named… [omitted for privacy]…was my friend. He is dead. I put him in a body bag one sunny day, April 29, 1969. We'd been talking only a few minutes before he was shot about what we were going to do when we got back to the world. Now this was a guy who had come in country the same time as myself. A guy who was loveable and generous. He had blue eyes and sandy blond hair.

When he talked it was a soft drawl. He was a hick and he knew it. That was part of his charm. He didn't care. Man, I loved this guy like the brother I never had. But, I screwed up. I got too close to him. Maybe I didn't know any better. But I broke one of the unwritten rules of war. Don't get too close to people who are going to die. Sometimes you can't help it.

You hear vets use the term 'buddy' when they refer to a guy they spent the war with. "Me and this buddy of mine."

'Friend' sounds too intimate, doesn't it? "Friends" calls up images of being close. If he's a friend, then you're going to be hurt if he dies and war hurts enough without adding to the pain. Get close; get hurt. It's as simple as that.

In war you learn to keep people at that distance my wife talks about. You become so good at it that twenty years after the war you still do it without thinking. You won't allow yourself to be vulnerable again.

My wife knows two people who can get into that soft spot inside me. My daughters. I know it probably bothers her that they can do this. It's not that I don't love my wife. I do. She's put up with a lot from me. She'll tell you that when she signed on for better or worse she had no idea there was going to be so much of the latter. But with my daughters it's different.

My girls are mine. They'll always be my kids. Not marriage, not distance, not even death can change that. They are something on this earth that can never be taken away from me. I belong to them. Nothing can change that. I can have an ex-wife; but my girls can never have an ex-father. There's the difference.

I can still see the faces though they all seem to have the same eyes.

When I think of us I always see a line of dirty grunts sitting on a paddy dike. We're caught in the first gray silver between darkness and light. That first moment when we know we've survived another night and the business of staying alive for one more day is about to begin. There was so much hope in that brief space of time. It's what we used to pray for. 'One more day, God. One more day.'

And I can hear our conversations as if they'd only just been spoken. I still hear the way we sounded, the hard cynical jokes, our morbid sense of humor. We were scared to death of dying and trying our best not to show it.

I recall the smells too. Like the way cordite hangs on the air after a fire fight. Or the pungent odor of rice paddy mud. So different from the black dirt of Iowa. The mud of Nam smells ancient somehow. Like it's always been there. And I'll never forget the way blood smells, slick and drying on my hands. I spent a long night that way once. That memory isn't going anywhere.

I remember how the night jungle appears almost dream like as the pilot of a Cessna buzzes overhead, dropping parachute flares until morning. That artificial sun would flicker and make shadows run through the jungle.

It was worse than not being able to see what was out there sometimes. I remember once looking at the man next to me as a flare floated overhead. The shadows around his eyes were so deep that it looked like his eyes were gone. I reached over and touched him on the arm; without looking at me he touched my hand. 'I know man. I know.' That's what he said.

'I know man.' And at that moment he did.

God I loved those guys. I hurt every time one of them died. We all did. Despite our posturing. Despite our desire to stay disconnected, we couldn't help ourselves. I know why Tim O'Brien writes his stories. I know what gives Bruce Weigle the words to create poems so honest I cry at their horrible beauty. It's love. Love for those guys we shared the experience with.

We did our jobs like good soldiers, and we tried our best not to become as hard as our surroundings. We touched each other and said, 'I know.' Like a mother holding a child in the middle of a nightmare. 'It's going to be all right." We tried hard not to lose touch with humanity. We tried to walk that line. To be the good boys our parents had raised and not to give into that unnamed thing we knew was inside us all.

You want to know what frightening is? It's a nineteen-year-old boy who's had a sip of that power over life and death that war gives you.

It's a boy who, despite all the things he's been taught, knows that he likes it. It's a nineteen-year-old boy who's just lost a friend and is angry and scared and determined that, 'Some @#*s<> gonna pay.' To this day the thought of that boy can wake me from a sound sleep and leave me staring at the ceiling.

As I write this, I have a picture in front of me. It's of two young men. On their laps are tablets. One is smoking a cigarette. Both stare without expression at the camera. They're writing letters. Staying in touch with places they would rather be. Places and people they hope to see again.

The picture shares space in a frame with one of my wife. She doesn't mind. She knows she's been included in special company. She knows I'll always love those guys who shared that part of my life, a part she never can.

And she understands how I feel about the ones I know are out there yet. The ones who still answer the question, 'When were you in Vietnam?' 'Hey, man. I was there just last night.' "

Forwarded by:

Terry Rigney
Webmaster for 3rd Battalion, 27th Marines
Web site.

CHAPTER EIGHT

Time for a Parade?

1985-1986

By the mid-eighties I finally hit my stride. I had finally adapted to the new paradigm in the corporate world and focused my attention and skills on the midsize to large companies. It was there I felt I could be the most effective. By helping them grow I knew that I could become a valuable asset. I had not attained the full success I wanted but I knew I was on my way in my chosen profession. At that time I was working for a large national corporation. They provided services to companies of all sizes, everything from computerized payroll services, accounts receivable, accounts payable, tax management, unemployment compensation management, HR reports and financial statements.

I joined the company before the time when they reached a billion dollars in sales. Once they achieved that milestone they immediately started to change. When I first came on board they were exclusively looking for gunfighters. They were eager to open accounts and establish themselves as the premier service provider in the country. I was given a territory and allowed to sell all related payroll products, except for the accounting services, to any company regardless of size. If I were to uncover an opportunity for those accounting services I would bring in the appropriate team and would receive compensation if the deal was closed. Once again it was a commission-only job but the commission you were paid on the sale and the set-up was high and you received an on-going royalty each month based on the billing to your customer base.

After the billion-dollar mark was reached the territories were cut down and the companies you could sell to were categorized and restricted by size and industry. The sales force had increased five-fold and the new hires coming in would not receive the same high compensation as those of us who had helped build the company. In defense of the company I must say that for a while we old-timers were being treated well. I still had the original territory I started with. I had been given the west and south sides of Chicago that were previously considered training territories. They were not considered to be as lucrative as downtown territories or the sexy new and affluent suburbs with their emerging corporate headquarters (driven out of Chicago by the crippling high taxes imposed on them by the city) and burgeoning commercial corridors. Through the tenacity I had learned in the Marine Corps and my now vast sales experience I managed to turn these previously unproductive areas into "President's Club" territories. That meant I had not only achieved one hundred percent of the sales quota I was given, but I exceeded it. This had never been done in those areas. For my effort I was well compensated and attended their President's Club meetings, which were held at all-expense-paid trips for me and my wife to such resorts as Boca Raton Florida, San Francisco, and Maui.

The company had once been a great place to work and afforded the true gunfighter the freedom and opportunity to make things happen. But now that things were changing I could see the writing on the wall. They didn't really need heavy hitters with large incomes anymore. They had become a household name virtually destroying or buying out all competition. One out of seven American workers were having their payroll checks processed by them and that number was growing. With all this growth came a new corporate attitude and a new management team. The social rules of the corporate culture were invading this utopia. The criteria for success and income was changing from how much you sold each week to how many times you went out for a drink with the boss. Your future could also be determined by how often you played golf with the right manager and how many weekends you could go skiing or play paint ball.

I knew this new shift was not for me. Despite all the years I had been there I really had no close friends at the company. I would go out for a drink after our weekly sales meetings with the rest of the salesmen but the conversations were almost exclusively work related. I noticed as time went by fewer and fewer of the old-timers I started with were still around. A few of them were some of the greatest salesmen

I've ever known. Even though I admired them greatly I was still living by the rules of engagement I learned in Vietnam: "Don't get too close." I had a wife, three daughters, my sisters and their families and two friends, Dennis and Paul. I didn't want to let more people into my life. I resisted going out to events where there were people I did not know. This was a tremendous burden for my wife who was, by nature, outgoing and fun loving. She wound up going to many functions by herself.

Although I was withdrawn in my social settings I wouldn't admit I had a problem or even talk about it. I thought discussing any personal problems was a sign of weakness. I would walk into a room of people and immediately think to myself, "I wonder if they know what I know? I wonder if they know what I've seen or what I've done?" Then I would think, "Who cares?" When I did find myself in a social setting I would generally be very quiet and observant, studying those around me. People who witnessed me in those moments would be surprised to find out I was in sales. I didn't fit their concept of a loud, slick, smooth-talking salesman.

By this time I had three daughters: Deana Christine, Lisa Marie and Allison Joy. I strongly regret I wasn't able to express the full joy and love I had for them and ask them to forgive me for that. I wish I could have been more involved in their young lives but I found myself struggling to come to grips with who I was. This is no excuse but I knew I was not affording them the same kind of nourishing that I had received from my family. Each one of them has grown to be quite exceptional, with the similar characteristics of goodness and kindness, along with their own individual strengths as well.

Deana has the confidence of an eldest child. She is organized with a good sense of business, logic and determination, and had a successful sales career before giving it up to care for her husband and beautiful children, Samantha and Jake. She is intelligent, solid and reliable with a good heart.

Lisa is sensitive and compassionate. She is the peacemaker that puts aside her own self-interest without hesitation for those in need. If it wasn't for Lisa I would not be alive today. It is her kidney inside me that saved my life. She is a loving wife and has three beautiful daughters, Devyn, Lizzie, and stepdaughter Karly.

Allison came along later in my life. She arrived at a time when the struggling was getting less and I had more time to spend with her physically and emotionally. She became very outgoing and the center of attention, taking the lead roles in high school plays and developing a confident personality. She also has three beautiful children, Abbey, Aiden and Aaron.

I am fortunate to see my daughters and grandchildren frequently to this day. I love them very much and rely on their love and support. Each of them is a wonderful, loving parent, and I believe their stories are still unfolding and wish them all the happiness that is possible for them to achieve.

The decision to go or stay at my job was taken out of my hands. I made the mistake of telling a fellow employee that I had no use for the new management team and their new philosophy. I thought them to be weak and basically just a bunch of bean counters without a clue. This fellow employee took it upon himself to go to the new manager and relay my description of him and his team. It didn't take long for the new manager to give this dinosaur of a salesman my two-week notice. I left with a nice severance package and never looked back

It was during this time that Dennis was going out on his own in his musical career. Tommy Shaw decided to leave Styx for a while to pursue a solo career. Dennis did not want to replace Tommy so he held his place open in Styx and tried his hand at doing some solo work also. His first album, "Desert Moon," was a critical success. The title track landed in the top ten and the album went gold. Hard on the heels of that success he proceeded to record his second album. In 1985 he had seen a special on PBS about the dedication of the Vietnam Veterans Memorial in Washington, D.C. This moved him to write a song about Vietnam. He started with the words "I was lucky you know, I wasn't there I didn't have to go and face my fear." From that was born the song "Black Wall" and the album *Back to the World*. It was not only about veterans returning to the United States and finding it hard to assimilate. It was also about a rock star who had been with a highly successful rock band and was trying to re-enter the rock world by himself.

The album started to make its way through the veterans' community. In interviews Dennis gave to the media he mentioned the fact that I, his friend and brother-in-law, was a wounded Vietnam veteran and he had gotten some idea of who we were through me. Since I had not joined any veterans' organizations or been active in the veterans' community I was not known in those circles.

An event was planned at a downtown Chicago restaurant to announce the official release of the album *Back to the World* and Dennis invited my wife and me to attend. The press was there and after the appropriate interviews and pictures we settled down to order dinner. As we waited for our food we were approached by several men. One of them introduced himself as Phil Meyer. He said he was on the organizing committee of the Chicago Vietnam Veterans Welcome Home Parade. Dennis looked at me and I told him I had never heard of the committee or any parade. To be honest my first thought was this guy had a few cards short of a full deck. He said he wanted to meet us and if it was alright he would like to talk to us for a few minutes after dinner. Dennis said it would be okay and Phil went back to the table with his associates.

He must have been watching us closely for after our dessert and in the middle of my second cup of coffee, he came over by himself and asked permission to pull up a chair and join us. He told Dennis he was a big fan and when he shook my hand he said, "Welcome home." I stuttered and said, "Thank you." I felt a shudder run through my body. I was filled with unexplainable emotion and had to blink back tears. No one but my family and neighbors had said that to me since that day in 1968 on 117th Street. Now, almost eighteen years later it hit me like an unexpected jolt of electricity. All at once I had feelings of sadness, pride, loss and a sense that this man had invaded my sanctum sanctorum. I was doing fine keeping those emotions locked up inside and now with those two words this stranger had thrown open the door.

Phil began by saying his real job was with the Veterans Administration as a team leader in a veterans outreach program. He held sessions where veterans would come to discuss their feelings about the war and he would act as a facilitator in helping them get assistance with such things as benefits, education, jobs and mental health issues like PTSD (post traumatic stress disorder). I had heard of these outreach centers but once again I believed that to seek assistance would be an act of weakness. Phil went on to explain that a few veterans were planning to have a welcome home parade in Chicago the next year. He said he and a group of Chicago veterans had gone to a parade the year before in New York City. The parade there drew twenty-five thousand marchers and he said he couldn't begin to tell the tremendous effect it had not only on the marchers but also on the crowds that lined the streets to watch them. He went on to say a man named Tom Stack had come back to Chicago and was convinced the time was right to heal a nation that was so divided by hate and distrust. He believed Chicago, in the heartland of America, was the perfect city to hold the definitive parade that could accomplish this healing. They did some research and found there were about six hundred fifty thousand Vietnam era veterans within driving distance of Chicago.

He went on to say the plans called for a series of events, one of which was to be a concert in Grant Park. He said they were trying to get some main acts and they were hoping Dennis would consider performing. Dennis told him he would like to find out more about it before he made up his mind. Phil said he appreciated that and then turned to me. He handed me his card and said he would like to talk to me further to see if I would be interested in joining the committee. I thanked him and said this sounded like a major project and I had a full-time, demanding job as well as a wife and children. He smiled and said, "That's all right, we all have jobs and families." With that he got up and left the restaurant.

Dennis turned to me and asked what I thought. I told him to be careful until I checked it out. I never heard of this group before but that didn't mean too much. I had not been a part of the veterans' community. Except for Paul, from whom I had moved across the street in Mokena, Illinois and Dennis, I had not even discussed the war in any detail. I belonged to no veterans' organizations at that time and thought I had done a pretty good job of keeping the experience deep inside until someone I didn't know said those two innocuous words, "Welcome Home," that nearly brought me to tears.

That night, with some trepidation, I called Phil. I told myself I was doing it to protect Dennis from getting involved in something that might not be on the up and up. In reality I was greatly intrigued. Could this be possible? Was anyone still interested? Hadn't we all made the decision to just let it go? Did I have the energy to immerse myself in those memories once again? What would be the point? Phil sounded genuinely pleased that I called and said there was a meeting at an office in downtown Chicago on 55 West Monroe Street that Saturday and invited me to attend. He said he would tell the others I would be there and looked forward to seeing me again.

I found the building and the suite where the meeting was being held. The suite was being donated by a brokerage firm named, Jeffries and Company, Inc. Phil met me at the door. He said there already had been several meetings at the homes of various volunteers and this meeting was to distribute specific tasks to individuals. He said he told Tom and the committee about me and I would be offered a role in this endeavor. He introduced me to Tom Stack. Tom was tall and slender and had an aura of strength and confidence.

The parade was his brain child. Tom served as a sergeant with the 9th Army Infantry Division where he received two silver stars. He was currently teaching law as a professor at Daley College in Chicago. Tom exuded passion and bright eyed determination. He carried himself as the combat infantry non-com officer he had been and through his very presence demanded attention and respect.

I was also introduced to Gene Conolly, Roger McGill and Julio Gonzalez. Gene was a lawyer and handled the legal aspects of the group. Roger was a mid-level executive at Illinois Bell Telephone and Julio was a maintenance engineer for General Motors. They had gone to the parade in New York and had been greatly affected. I met some more of the inner circle: Angelo Terrell, assistant director of the United States Department of Labor; Connie Edwards, a nurse who had served in Vietnam; Larry Langowski, another Illinois Bell executive; and Ken Plummer, a retired army colonel who had served in World War II, Korea and Vietnam. There were other veterans in attendance who seemed eager and excited as they introduced themselves. There were whites, blacks, Hispanics, men and women alike and it became immediately apparent to me that there was no class, race or gender distinctions here as there was none in Vietnam. I knew instinctively that this was not a phony attempt at political correctness or social engineering. These were lessons learned in war. It didn't matter the color or background of a person. It only mattered that you could trust the person next to you. Not to close a deal or get a promotion or help you make a touchdown, but to be able to put your life in their hands without thinking about it.

Tom stood at the front of the room and asked everyone to settle down and take a seat. He introduced himself and began to speak. He was the perfect combination of combat soldier, Chicagoan, gentleman and motivator. He started by saying that he, along with others present, had attended the New York City parade and that it was greeted with enthusiasm and emotion from thousands of bystanders lining Broadway. He said it was on the way home that he got the inspiration to organize a parade in Chicago.

My first thought was, "Right, we're so pathetic we have to throw our own welcome home parade." I was about one minute away from getting up and leaving when the passion and conviction in his voice started to have a confining effect on me and I began to feel riveted to my seat. He said he was consumed with the idea that the time had come to heal our nation. He said the fault was not only in those who protested against us but also in ourselves by letting others define us and keeping our service, pride and love for our country buried deep inside us. He stated his goal was to attract one hundred thousand marchers to the streets of Chicago. That was about the time my mind started wandering again. I kept thinking over and over again, "One hundred thousand marchers? How is this going to happen?" Tom said he had already gotten permits for next June. That meant we would have a little less than a year to do this.

As far as I could tell everyone there had a full-time job. Who would have time to undertake such an enormous project as this? Where was the money to come from? There had been no talk yet about city or corporate sponsorship. I heard nothing about any plans or budget for advertising. Did anyone here have any experience in doing something like this? I half expected Judy Garland and Mickey Rooney to bust out in the room and say, "Hey guys! Let's put on a major Broadway show in the barn!" As a business man I felt my heart sink as the meeting progressed without addressing any of these issues. It was like, Tom said it so it must be so. No one could deny the fire and passion in Tom but I felt that his confidence was going to be an acquired taste.

On the positive side I was pleased to see that all the people I had met so far were gainfully employed. There were no "professional veterans" as I had originally feared. There was a segment of the veteran community that used their experiences to try to gain some sort of advantage by portraying themselves as victims or going around bragging about things they had not done. There were even those who had never served in Vietnam, like one of the founders of Vietnam Veterans Against the War, who went about as if they had.

In the early stages of the parade a screening process was developed. This process was effectively able to expose one person, who claimed he had been a prisoner in the infamous Hanoi Hilton, as a fraud. I was relieved when Phil asked me to bring my DD214, amended, to the meeting. The DD214 is a discharge record from the service showing where and when you served, medals and citations awarded and your MOS. My amended DD214 read: PFC Charles S. Lofrano; United States Marine Corps; Republic of Vietnam; MOS-0331 Infantry Machine Gunner; Related Civilian Occupation, Weapons; Commendations, Purple Heart, Combat Action Ribbon, Presidential Unit Citation, National Defense Medal, Vietnam Service Medal with one Bronze Star, Vietnam Campaign Medal, Republic of Vietnam Meritorious Unit Citation(Gallantry Cross Colors with Palm and Frame) and Republic of Vietnam Meritorious Unit Citation (Civil Action Color with Palm and Frame). It had also been amended to show I had been permanently medically retired in 1974 and that my discharge was honorable.

I focused back on what Tom was saying when I heard him mention my name. He reintroduced me to the group and told them I was to be in charge of the concert that was to be held at the Petrillo Band Shell in Grant Park. I was stunned! Had I missed something? When was this decided? When I was first approached by Phil I thought my primary mission was to convince Dennis to be a part of the event. As the group applauded the announcement, Tom looked at me and asked me to stay after the meeting. From the moment I met him I thought there was something compelling about Tom. When he talked to you he looked directly in your eyes and you felt his strength and commitment. He was not what you would consider to be a bully but he had an air of inevitability about him that made you believe that nothing could stand in his way. You sensed this was a great man yet humble in his respect for others. It has always been clear to me that he was the only man who could have pulled this thing off with what we had to work with. He had that leadership thing, the visionary who dreamed of impossible things and then turned them into reality. Someone who would not suffer fools and would only choose those who he thought could contribute to the overall objective without excuses. He was the kind of man you would follow into hell. There were only a few people on earth whose approval of me was important. He was one of them.

After the meeting Tom, Phil and I sat around Tom's desk. Tom looked over my DD214 and asked about my family and how I felt about Vietnam. I told him my family was very important to me and that I had come to deal with my war experiences. He gave me a knowing smile and continued. He explained some of the problems they were having with the parade. He said one of the biggest problems was financing the event. The city of Chicago had pledged a certain amount of money but for whatever reason had thus far only released a small portion. There were no great amounts of corporate money coming in either. Coors Beer had pledged they would do something but that was about it. Tom felt the lack of support was for several reasons. First and foremost was the controversy over the war itself. It was still not politically correct as evidenced by the media, who refused to honor those who had fought and continued to portray them as losers, drug users and psychopaths. This, he said, was also the major reason for the parade. Next he said we had little credibility. No one could believe anything of this proposed magnitude could ever happen especially with no media or major entertainment support. Lastly, Tom believed there was a lot of public guilt about how the Vietnam veterans were treated when they got home and they were as reluctant as we were to bring up old wounds. To Tom, this last reason was as important as all the others.

He saw the parade as a national time of healing. Our back and forth exchange seemed to satisfy Tom about me but I was still a little unsure about the whole project. Whether he sensed this or not he went on to address what he had in mind for me. Due to the lack of city and corporate sponsorship thus far they were organizing fund raisers at the local community level to keep paying the phone bills, buying postage and printing brochures. He acknowledged this would never be enough. He believed he could get substantial corporate sponsorship if we could attract some famous entertainers to perform at the Petrillo Band Shell in Grant Park after the parade and the following day. He said he had assigned that task to someone else and although he had promised such names as James Brown and the Temptations, nothing had materialized. Tom wanted me to take his place. He said my experience in business and my relationship with Dennis together with the fact that I had written some songs qualified me, in his mind, to do the job.

He went on to clarify by saying that as a business man I had made presentations to large corporations which would help in making pitches for corporate sponsorship and my limited association with the music industry was the closest thing they had to an insider. He didn't say this, but I'm sure another reason was that he believed my inclusion would help to guarantee Dennis's participation. He wanted me to produce the concert, book the acts and sell the package to prospective sponsors. He had a few acts he insisted should be included. There were a couple of bands made up of Vietnam veterans who were recognizable in the veterans community and played for many veterans benefits. There was also a singer who had been on Armed Forces Radio Network in Vietnam that brought a little bit of hope to our troops stationed there. Other than these, I was free to book whomever I thought would be good and attract some sponsors.

I told him it would be tricky booking the acts. I wouldn't know if I could offer them any money until I sold the idea to the sponsors and I couldn't sell it to the sponsors until I had the acts. Without changing his expression he looked at me and said, "Oh yeah, one more thing. I'd also like you to negotiate with the various city agencies you'll need to put on the concert at Petrillo, like, parks, streets and sanitation, city hall and the appropriate unions."

This was all truly overwhelming to say the least. I re-stated the obvious and reminded Tom I had an exacting job and a growing family. He again reminded me they all had jobs and families. I asked if I could think about it and get back to him. He looked disappointed, as if I should have the same enthusiasm as he did. I sensed this and told him he could surely give me a couple of days to wrap myself around an idea he had been thinking about for a couple of years. He smiled and said that was a good answer. He appreciated my caution and asked if I could call him on Monday with my answer. I said I would and left as Tom and Phil continued to talk.

My mind was reeling as I drove home and I barely remember the trip. Booking the performers and producing the concert might be fun even though I had never done anything like it before and there was no money yet to do it. I was less sure of the other part of my assignment. Mostly I was questioning this entire endeavor. Who was I to be apart of something like this? Was this really even necessary? I had spent over seventeen years trying to convince myself that the war and what happened after had no effect on me. Every time those feelings came up I would be dragged down into terrible fits of depression and despair. I would drive by open fields and try to figure out how far a tree line was from me and where would be a good place to set up an ambush. I would search for a false horizon and scan the tops of trees for snipers. I never wanted to admit it but every aspect of my life was affected by my war experiences. When I first got home and people noticed my arm, (first in a cast and then wrapped in a supportive bandage), I usually told them I had broken my arm in a skiing accident, or I jumped out of the window mere seconds before "her" husband came home. I had finally managed to keep these emotions deep inside and came to terms with my demons to live a somewhat normal, successful life.

How could I now become a part of something that was sure to bring up all those feelings again not only for myself but thousands of other veterans and their families? Would the parade exorcise those demons or just further hide them? As hard as I tried to talk myself out of this mission there was something deep inside that kept telling me it had to be done.

That Monday, after I talked to my wife and gained her support, I called Tom and told him I would do it. With that agreement I started on another odyssey that would bring me great joy and at the same time great feelings of sorrow and pain.

As the days of planning went on it was just as I had feared. All the memories and emotions of the war and the struggle to adjust to life in the world came rushing back with full force. I would find myself crying at times for no apparent reasons and felt so weak and ashamed that I dared not tell anyone about it. There were days when I would be immobilized, unable to move from the sofa. I would call work and tell them I was working out of the house, but I would barely be checking my messages. At the same time I kept thinking about the veterans I had run into in the course of my job. Many of us downplayed our military experience or completely deleted it from our resumes. As a result a kind of underground was created especially in the professional world where you were more likely to run into university graduates who were against the war and marched in protest against it and us. I'll never forget the look on a bright eyed fellow female co-worker one day when she learned I was a Vietnam veteran. She smugly mentioned that I was one of "those" that she and her friends had helped by protesting the war and finally bringing us home. I looked at her and without skipping a beat said, "Oh, you're one of 'those' that convinced our enemies to keep fighting and killing us when we had beaten them on the battlefield." It was if I had just slapped her across the face. Needless to say we never got along after that.

Incidents such as these caused us to be cautious in what we said to our fellow workers or in my case, to prospective clients. You could penetrate the underground by using certain phrases or observing certain attitudes. For instance, I had been trying to get into a very large account for several months. I knew I could provide the products and services they needed and felt confident my company was up to the task. One day I asked the data processing manager if there was anything he needed or wanted to do his job but was unable to get from his current vendors in a timely fashion. He acknowledged there was some special software he was looking for. I asked if I could help him with this, would he give me an appointment to present the capabilities, products and services of my company. He said he would and I was able to perform the task in a timely fashion. I went to his office to drop off the software personally. His secretary said he wasn't in so I asked her if I could leave the software with her. She said yes and I left one of my cards with the package. On the back of the card I wrote the words, "Mission Accomplished."

    The next day he called me to thank me and to set up an appointment. When we agreed on the date he hesitatingly asked me if I had been in the service, because of how I had signed my card. I told him I had been and went over my service history. By the end of our conversation I learned that he had also been in the marines and fought in Vietnam in 1968 with 1st Recon. He had been wounded and received the Silver Star at the Battle of Hue City. I did business with him for many years introducing new and efficient technology to his organization and becoming good friends along the way.

Another time, I walked into the office of the COO of a major corporation and on the wall was a picture of Jane Fonda. She was smiling broadly while sitting behind an enemy anti-aircraft gun that was used to shoot down and kill American servicemen. The picture was in the center of a bull's-eye and across the top were written the words, "Hanoi Jane". I knew I found a friend. He had served with the 173rd and seen heavy combat. We developed a mutual trust and respect immediately.

In addition to my regular clients, I started handling government accounts; federal, state and local. Municipalities were just making the move to local and wide area networks. I noticed most of them were putting employees in charge of the change who had no technical expertise. This was the case until I called on a medium-sized village in a southeastern suburb of Chicago. The person in charge of data processing had an interesting background. He retired from the village police force after twenty years. He taught himself computer and network technology and was one of the most knowledgeable people in that field I had met at the time. Another interesting fact was he had served in the navy in Vietnam in 1968. He was with the Tiensha Security Police and patrolled the deep harbor at Tiensha near Da Nang. He managed his village into one of the most up-to-date, state of the art municipalities around, acting as an example for others to follow.

I thought of these men as I contemplated my potential participation in the parade. They, and others like them I met, were good, honest men who were at the top of their fields. They deserved to have their stories and successes told to counter the distortions by others who did not serve. They deserved to be held up as role models and honored for what they had done for us and what they had overcome. Thinking of these former warriors made my decision easier.

When a war is vilified as much as Vietnam was and the reasons for the war are summarily dismissed by many who refused to give up their comfort and safety to serve, all that is left is the horror, the body count, the destruction, the civilian casualties and the loss of innocence by those who fought it. Imagine if World War II had not been recognized as a just war. How would Americans have come to terms with the two hundred ninety thousand-plus American deaths or the six hundred seventy thousand non-mortal wounded? How would we have dealt with the millions of civilian casualties? What could we say about the fire bombing of Dresden, the bombing of Berlin or the destruction of Hiroshima and Nagasaki? In planning for the parade I had to deal with these resurgent feelings and put my heart and soul into the success of it. Good God, I hoped Tom was right!

If you were to walk into the parade office during those hectic planning days you would have no idea what was going on. Physically it looked like a regular office suite. A large area with desks lined up in order. There were a few offices on the perimeter and a conference room. That, however, was where the similarity ended. People were constantly coming in and out. Some were dressed in business suits and some in old army fatigues. Some had short cropped haircuts while others sported long hair, ponytails and beards. There were a few computers and only four telephones. The first impression that leapt into my mind was one of chaos. One of the first things I learned was there seemed to be no coordination of tasks among the people in charge of their own specific areas. Tom chose the person who was to be in charge of each specific aspect of the parade. He told them exactly what he expected them to accomplish and then left them to their own devices on how to get it done.

He called several meetings during the week to review reports on the progress. His style was to praise those who were making headway and could show results. He would rarely get angry. He could generally show his disappointment by merely withholding his praise. No one wanted to disappoint Tom.

Since we all had full-time jobs we couldn't attend all the frequent meetings that Tom held. As a result there was not a lot of fraternizing between the principals. There were those who had the responsibility to organize the marchers and those who planned the parade route. Someone had to coordinate with the hotels and restaurants. The city and state organizations had to be kept up-to-date.

There were local fundraisers to be organized and veteran groups to be contacted. The media had to be courted and on and on. I would hear bits and pieces of the progress of the other parts of the parade but I can honestly say I never had the entire picture. I put my trust in the others as I had done with my brothers in Vietnam and concentrated on my part of the operation. As a result, to this day, I cannot personally recall everyone that was involved and I profoundly apologize to them for not being able to mention all their particular contributions by name. I do know that many people contributed at least as much and in many cases more than I did. I have listed the names of the committee members at the end of this book. Once again I apologize to any I have omitted. I believe that Tom and maybe Phil were the only ones who knew exactly everything that was going on at any given time.

Through the veteran grapevine I tried to find out what corporations were sympathetic to veterans' causes or who had veterans in top positions in their companies As I made my pitch to these selected companies I was treated with kindness and respect but the answer was always the same. Since I couldn't commit to big name acts and we weren't getting much media coverage we lacked the credibility needed to garner financial backing. Thank God for WGN (the local Chicago television station), the *Chicago Tribune* and Bill Kurtis from CBS, channel two in Chicago. They were starting to spread the word and without them we really would have been dead in the water. In addition to Bill there was Rick Kogan from the *Tribune*, a great friend and long time supporter who I knew personally and another *Tribune* writer Anne Keegan whom I never had the privilege of meeting. I was told that Tom made the rounds to all the local media and WGN was the first to acknowledge the possibility of covering the parade. This is not to denigrate the other local stations. It was a difficult call for those affiliates to make a commitment to what many thought was a quixotic quest. WGN was the hometown station. Even if it turned out to be a small gathering it could be covered as a local event.

While I was trying to raise some corporate funds I was also trying to book some entertainers. Dennis had agreed to perform at the concert in Grant Park following the parade. He was starting to promote his solo album and the difficult task of separating himself from Styx. Once you heard his voice you immediately recognized him but he couldn't advertise himself as Styx so it took educating the public as to who he was. So although Styx sold tens of millions of albums primarily on Dennis's writing and singing, it would take a while to establish himself as a solo artist which he finally did with great success.

Other than Dennis, who was a great asset, and the unknown artists from the veterans' community, I had nothing. I got a list of agencies that handled the types of acts I knew could attract media attention. Unfortunately they would agree to play for their regular fees of anywhere from twenty-five to one hundred thousand dollars. I took the information back to the corporations I had previously contacted and presented them with the proposition of sponsoring the acts and being assured of getting the credit.It was then I realized the problem was not the acts but rather the cause. If we were holding an event to raise money for widows and orphans of dead servicemen or money to help rebuild Vietnam or remove land mines and unexploded ordinance, great causes all, they might be interested. They just couldn't wrap their minds around the idea of holding a parade being billed as a "healing event" for our nation. When they put it that way, they almost convinced me.

After constantly hitting my head against a brick wall I decided to change my strategy. I had Dennis as the headliner and I knew when people realized who he was he would fill the Petrillo Band Shell in Grant Park. I then needed some hot local rock bands to play some sixties and seventies tunes that could get the crowd going. I also looked for some jazz and blues groups for which Chicago was famous. To these ends I let out the word that I would be accepting audition tapes for a large outdoor event in Grant Park promising great exposure for rising artists. I ultimately received dozens of demo tapes and was able to pick some very good bands. Now, with Dennis as the main attraction, a good assortment of local talent, the veterans bands and the designated speakers, the concert was set.

Dennis helped greatly by talking about the concert outside the state of Illinois. As he went around the country to promote his album he would bring up the parade and encourage veterans in the various audiences to come to Chicago on June 13 1986. Phil and I took this final plan to Coors and together we came to a compromise. Coors would contribute some money up front and in addition provide their beer at the concert. The proceeds would be donated to the parade committee for expenses. I had mixed feelings about this solution. I was happy that we had a commitment from a major sponsor but I realized it would all depend on how many people showed up.

With the concert and performers nailed down and the finances somewhat settled, I started on the next phase. Tom had gotten the permits for the Petrillo Band Shell but he had not negotiated with the Illinois Brotherhood of Electrical Workers. The "IBEW" Union had hard and fast rules about the access to electricity being handled exclusively by certified union members. There was obviously a charge for those services. Unfortunately the committee did not have the money to pay for them. I asked for a meeting with some of the union officials to request a waiver of those fees. Their spokesman said they were sympathetic but there was no way they could waive the fees.

They told me it would be dangerous for non-engineers to fiddle around with the intricacies of the power sources and energy grids. I agreed with him and said I wasn't proposing doing the electrical services without them. I was asking that they donate their time. I said we could put them up in hotels, feed them and give them backstage access.

During these negotiations we were interrupted by the arrival of a man surrounded by a small entourage. He was a slight, impeccably dressed African American. The acknowledgements he received from the union officials in the room indicated he was a powerful man. We were introduced and he was filled in as to what was going on. He listened intently and asked me to repeat what I wanted. After I repeated my request he told me how many people it would take to handle an event like this and what the normal fees would be. I again explained we had no money. He asked me what my participation in this was. I told him I was a wounded combat veteran and I believed in the need for this event. He asked me how much money I was making for this. I chuckled and told him truthfully that I, like the others on the committee, was receiving no money. He paused for a moment and the others in attendance waited for his reply. He said his brother was a Vietnam veteran and he knew we had gotten a raw deal. He also said many of the men in his chapter were also veterans and he was sure they would want to help. He looked around the table and said, "Give this man whatever he needs." With that he stood up, shook my hand and left. This was so surreal that to this day I am ashamed and embarrassed that I cannot recall the man's name. In my mind he will always be remembered as another angel sent by God.

Whether he was a real angel or not, after that meeting I had no problems dealing with the other various city agencies. I still had to get the band shell ready for the concert by providing chairs for the front rows, sound towers and speakers. These items would have to be obtained and set up. We got the chairs from the park district, the sound equipment was donated by a sound company and the set up would be done by volunteers. While I was dealing with these things the other plans were progressing. I learned that the parade route had been solidified. It was to run 2.8 miles through the streets of downtown Chicago, forming up at Olive Park (Olive Park was named after Milton Lee Olive the third, an African American soldier who received the Congressional Medal of Honor posthumously in Vietnam. In an extreme act of bravery he threw himself on a live hand grenade saving the lives of his fellow soldiers.).

The parade would then start off from Navy Pier, go west on Grand Avenue and then south on State Street to Wacker Drive. It would turn from Wacker Drive on to LaSalle, then to Jackson ending at Grant Park for the concert. Ironically it was in Grant Park that some of the most violent anti-war protests had taken place in 1968. I received a copy of the route but couldn't tell how it ultimately came to be.

I think Roger McGill was responsible for this as well as the placement of the marching units together with Phil and Tom. I knew that the army guys must have been in charge with the order of the march because I noticed the Marine Corps units were placed at the end of the parade. I jokingly acknowledged this to Tom and thanked him for saving the best for last. Hotels were set up to be used as headquarters for the various units that served in Vietnam. You could inquire as to which hotel housed your outfit. Whether you were in the Americal Division, the 1st or 3rd Marine Division, the 9th Infantry Division, the 25th, 173rd, 101st, 1st Air Cavalry or whatever, you could stay at a hotel where you could possibly be reunited with a war buddy from the past. There was also to be a registry where you could look up a person by name and find out where they were staying. A mailing list of twenty-five hundred veterans organizations was compiled and volunteers sent out notices and personally visited as many groups as they could in the Chicago area.

Tom wanted this to be a family affair so he was billing the festivities as a three-day event. It would include the parade and concert on Friday, a POW/MIA memorial in Daley Plaza followed by another afternoon concert on Saturday and a dinner on Saturday night for Medal of Honor recipients from WWII, Korea, and Vietnam at the Holiday Inn Mart Plaza. Sunday could be used as a leisurely day to tour the city and bid farewell to old comrades.

Several veterans from outside Chicago had constructed a scale model of the Vietnam Veterans Memorial known as "The Wall". It was the dedication of the wall in November of 1982 that started to change how people regarded the Vietnam veteran. Over one hundred thousand people had attended the dedication but as of the time of the parade most veterans had not seen it. As a result, two veterans built an exact replica built to scale displaying all the names of the fallen precisely as they were listed and arranged on the memorial in Washington. They were just beginning to tour the country with it. Tom wanted to have the "Traveling Wall" brought to Chicago to enhance the experience of the parade. He wanted to display it a week before and during the parade festivities. It was a great idea but we didn't have the money needed to pay these veterans to have the replica brought to Chicago. We needed to provide for their expenses including: travel, hotel, and meals.

I had been talking to Dennis about this and it was he who came up with the solution. He would perform a concert at the Park West to raise the funds needed to bring the wall to Chicago. Once again he charged no fee and not only brought the wall to Chicago, but also gave us much needed publicity as the concert was well covered by the Chicago media.

It seemed the plans were progressing but for every success there were five failures.

The city had promised seventy-five thousand dollars but had thus far only released twenty-five thousand. While Tom was estimating one hundred thousand marchers, no one in authority was taking him seriously and we were told we would only be getting five port-a-potties at Navy Pier. We were starting to get complaints from the residents of Lake Shore Drive that we were going to disrupt their area. They also were not too keen on the idea of loud rock music being played at the Petrillo Band Shell where they were used to hearing the wafting sounds of the Chicago Symphony Orchestra on a warm summer night. We were constantly short of funds and many of us were spending our own money and turning in receipts in the faint hope we might get reimbursed eventually. To top it off, we still had no idea of how many people would actually show up. My hope was that we would at least match the twenty-five thousand marchers who had showed up in New York while Tom was standing behind his prediction.

As the days of planning went on I suffered more from what I had originally feared. The memories and emotions were coming non-stop even as I tried to keep busy with my job, my family and the parade. As the parade got closer I was physically assisting in setting up chairs, sound equipment and the stage. My wife joined in our endeavors and was working with us on the phones and mailings. All these frantic activities, however, could not stop the feelings emerging from the dark place where

I thought I had successfully buried them. Vivid recollections of the sights, sounds and smells of combat filled my senses. The only feeling I would not succumb to was a feeling that I was a fool for what I had done. War is hell and no one knows this better than the warrior who fights it. Although I still felt guilty about leaving my brothers behind and wondered why I was alive while others were not, I never felt ashamed of what I did.

At the same time I was starting to understand why some would go to great lengths to avoid these experiences. The soldiers of the Revolutionary War would rather not have been at Valley Forge. Both Northerners and Southerners would rather not have been at Gettysburg. I'm sure if you asked the GIs on Normandy or Iwo Jima where they would rather be at the time I don't think they would have said it was dying on these beaches thousands of miles from home instead of being with their wives and children. If you see a Korean War veteran ,ask him if he would have preferred sitting by a warm fire with his loved ones instead of freezing in the snow in South Korea. We all would have preferred to pass the cup but we felt compelled to serve. To this day I still find it difficult to explain to those who don't understand it.

Then, all of a sudden, things began to change. The office was starting to get responses and inquiries almost constantly. It started to look like there would actually be people at the parade. I even started to feel confident about the twenty-five thousand number and some of the more optimistic of us were starting to predict as many as fifty thousand. I wasn't buying into that number; I was just happy to think there would be marchers and we weren't going to fail, that all the hard work and effort would not be in vain. We would gather our troops once again and we would celebrate our love for our country and our love for one another without fear with our heads held high. We could tell our countrymen that no matter what happened we loved them too and it was time to put aside our past and join together in friendship and common purpose. I knew this wouldn't be easy. The pain and the scars were deep but I knew it was time to try.

The week before the parade was very exciting. The hotels were starting to fill up. Veterans were coming to the parade office to get itineraries and check out what was going on. They were from Wisconsin, Indiana, Michigan, New York, Colorado, New Jersey, Florida, California, Iowa, Massachusetts, Ohio, Delaware, and more. There were even a few Australian veterans

In the midst of all this excitement I had a sudden thought about Tim, that forlorn soul I met so many years ago in the Great Lakes Naval Hospital. Somehow I hoped that wherever Tim was now he had heard about the parade. We were ready to come home. We had accepted ourselves and come to terms with our fellow citizens. I had the feeling that on this Friday the thirteenth a lot of old ghosts would be put to rest. I prayed that a lot of Tims would take the risk and join us on the streets of Chicago.

> "Sound the bugle boys for a twenty-one gun salute.
> Call for the ticker tape and assemble all the troops.
> Not a word about dominoes or the horrors of napalm.
> Let Johnny come marching home
> and greet him with a prayer and a song.
> For the boys of Vietnam."
>
> "Black Wall"
> From the Album
> Back to the World
> by
> Dennis DeYoung

CHAPTER NINE

Welcome Home

Chicago Illinois
Friday, June 13, 1986

    I left the Ambassador East Hotel in downtown Chicago at 6:00 on the morning of June 13, 1986. It had been raining all week. The local weathermen had predicted that this day was the only clear and sunny day we were to have for the foreseeable future. God bless those Chicago prognosticators. They came through and presented us with a glorious morning and evidence of a clear and beautiful day to come. Our plans had been germinating for over a year and it would have been daunting to be thwarted by the weather but it turned out that Sky Pilot Number One was giving us a husk and I was very grateful.
    I hardly remember the elevator ride down to the lobby or hailing a cab at the front entrance of that grand and historical hotel. I was halfway to the Petrillo Band Shell in Grant Park before the full impact hit me. After months of frustrating despair interspersed with fleeting glimpses of hope, the day had finally arrived. "The Chicago Vietnam Veterans Welcome Home Parade" had on this day passed from hope to reality. Friday the thirteenth had been a carefully chosen day. For those of us who had fought in Vietnam, survived the carnage and, with a great deal more difficulty, drawn an uneasy truce with our fellow countrymen,

it was an appropriate date. To everyone else Friday the thirteenth was a day to avoid, a superstitious segment of time when most people make plans and decisions only if forced to. For us it was the perfect day. It told a lot about us. Although our ranks consisted of all levels of American life from skid row derelicts and prison inmates to presidents of industry and members of Congress, for the most part we were a closed society. The parade was designed to help change this. No one really believed that one parade on one day could magically accomplish this task, but the idea was that it would be a start.

I thought of these things in the cab as I stared out the window. I also thought of the people I had left back at the Ambassador East Hotel that morning. None of them were Vietnam veterans but each had supported the veteran community and helped make this day happen and one of them had served above and beyond the call of duty. Pam, my wife of sixteen years at that time (thirty-eight years at the time of the writing of this book), was a representative of all our wives and families. Those who had stood by us though they hadn't seen what we had seen or done the things we had done. Those who were asked to understand the impossible and live with our nightmares and depressions. Those who were asked to perform the normal everyday tasks of civilized social intercourse while giving us time to heal ourselves when we desperately needed those reasons. We arranged the parade so that family members could march with their warriors but we knew this was small recognition for their selfless service.

Also back at the Ambassador East was Dennis with his wife, Suzanne, and Rick Kogan. I've chronicled Dennis's many contributions to this effort. He has been a great friend to the veteran community and closer than a brother to me over the years. I'm sure this is the first time many people have heard about his involvement in this historic event. He helped us, for no pay and little acknowledgement, at a time when it wasn't cool to support the troops. Rick Kogan has also been a friend of mine for many years. As an important writer and editor for the Chicago Tribune as well as an accomplished author, Rick's life has always been pretty full. Even so, he has always been there when we needed help and continues to this day to be one of our staunchest supporters. It was hard in the beginning to gain attention for our quest to put the parade on. Rick was one of the first prominent Chicago personalities along with Bill Kurtis to give us the credibility and respect we needed to ultimately deal with the various agencies and others in the media.

Before I left the hotel I had become a little concerned. I caught part of a morning news program that showed a reporter standing somewhere at Navy Pier saying that she didn't see any crowds and was predicting a light turn out for the parade. I tried not to concentrate on this report and kept thinking about all the activity of the last two weeks. It caused me a little stress but by the time I left the room and approached the elevator I had completely blocked it from my mind. My spirits picked up even more as I approached the band shell. I could see men in fatigues walking toward Navy Pier, crowded in cars hanging out the windows and honking their horns. There were hundreds of them and there definitely was an electric feeling in the air. I thought of the days leading up to the parade.

We had put the replica of the wall on Jackson and Michigan and I would stand there looking at all the names and seeing families going up to it together. Some were looking for the names of fallen comrades. Some were looking for the names of their fathers, brothers, sons and husbands. You could almost sense the relief coming through the sorrow and tears. I saw a father, on his knees in front of the wall, tell his children through tear-stained eyes about his fallen friend whose name was etched on the wall. As he held them closely I knew this was the first time this man had told his children about his time in Vietnam. If all we had accomplished were incidents like the one I witnessed at the wall between that father and his children as well as many others like it, and the happiness and exuberance of the men passing by me on their way to Navy Pier, I would consider this effort to be a success.

I was to open up the band shell and wait for some volunteers to help me get the place ready for the concert. No one knew exactly how many people would be marching yet or at what time the parade would end up at Grant Park so I wanted to be ready as early as possible to cover all contingencies. As I walked from the cab to the band shell I heard a rumble of motorcycle engines behind me. I turned to see what was going on just as the bikers were coming to a stop in front of me. There were about thirty of them dressed in fatigues with leather vests. One of them got off his bike and approached me. He asked me where Navy Pier was and I told him. He looked at me and for some reason asked if I was part of the parade. I told him that yes, I was the person putting on the concert after the parade was over and I hoped they would all come back to enjoy the music, food and beer. He came up to me, put his arms around me, hugged me and with tears in his eyes, the first of many I would see that day, thanked me. He also said that they would definitely be back and if there was anything they could do to help out, just to ask. I would use them later for stage security.

    I was waiting at the band shell for about an hour for my volunteers when all of a sudden my wife, Dennis and Suzanne pulled up. My wife came over to me crying and said she had some bad news. It seemed all the TV stations were now saying the turn out for the parade was going to be very light. She knew how much hard work I and the others had put into this and felt devastated for us since it now seemed it would be a failure. This didn't make sense to me. In the course of the hour I had been in front of the band shell I had first seen hundreds and later thousands of people make their way toward Navy Pier. Either the reporters were in the wrong place or I had been hallucinating. I just refused to believe this report so the three of them decided to check things out for themselves and said they would report back what they found out.

My volunteers finally showed up along with a few Chicago policemen. There was a meeting with Chicago's finest to coordinate activities and requests for coverage of certain areas one of which was the band shell. The IBEW workers who were assigned to us arrived and they began to prepare the stage. The first act was to be a patriotic performance by the Air Force Band. They would be the first contingent reaching Grant Park at the end of the parade so our first task was to set up enough chairs to accommodate them.

While the volunteers and electricians were busy on stage I went backstage to make sure everything was ready. Several restaurants donated food and drinks and they were being delivered. After the refreshments were stored away I sat down in the middle of the room. There was nothing more I could do. There was nothing more anyone could do. During the planning of the parade an army reserve officer came to the office to offer his assistance. His assessment was basically that we were so disorganized we had no chance of success. In a way he was almost right. As I sat there thinking about the last year I couldn't believe we had gotten this far. It was like the grunt's view of a war. He knew just what was going on directly in front of him, only dimly aware of the big picture. There were hundreds of people involved at all levels of the operation. More if you considered the volunteers and organizations that contributed their time. All these people, and I probably only knew fewer than a dozen by name.

Since we all had full-time jobs we had time to only concentrate on our duties and we were restricted by time to fraternize. I would see some of the participants briefly on my trips to the office and pick up bits and pieces of the entire puzzle. The thing that kept me going in this endeavor was the belief and trust in my comrades. Just as I instinctively knew who I could trust in combat, I knew who I could count on here, starting with Tom Stack.

I had come up with the schedule of performers. I built the performances around Dennis' spot. I put him in prime time to attract the most people who would drink the most Coors which would generate the most income to help pay off our debts. It would start with the Air Force Band followed by an invocation, some speeches by dignitaries and proceed from there. There was some flexibility to accommodate for the ultimate size of the crowd about which no one still had a clue.

The parade stepped off at 9:30. General William Westmoreland had agreed to be the grand marshal. He showed up in full uniform and ribbons, something he had not done for any gathering since he left the service. There was some concern as to what kind of reception he would receive from the veterans. Like everything else about Vietnam he had become controversial just by the fact of having been there and having to perform in impossible situations. "Westy," as we called him, led the parade together with Tom Stack and an honorary parade marshal named Jim Partridge. Jim was a Marine Corps veteran who lost both his legs in Vietnam. He made headline news a week before: While sitting in the backyard of his Chicago suburban home he heard a cry for help. It was from a child in the next yard who appeared to be drowning in a swimming pool. Jim threw himself out of his wheelchair and crawled over, and pulled the child out.

Due to the large amount of people showing up the parade jumped off a half hour early which was another fact to belie the early news reports. Just as the marchers were getting started, they were joined by Bob Wieland. Bob had been just about to sign a contract with the Philadelphia Phillies when he was drafted into the Army. In June of 1968 Bob, who became an Army medic, stepped on a land mine and lost both his legs at the hip. He just recently finished a three year "walk" from California to Washington, D.C. to raise money for world hunger. He had a specially tailored pad on his torso and pulled himself along with his hands. He came to Chicago because he desperately wanted to be a part of this historic event. When "Westy" saw him he insisted he take a place in front of the parade. These were the kind of men who came to Chicago that day.

Pam, Dennis and Suzanne had come back to the band shell to report the news media had been wrong. They were at LaSalle

Street when tens of thousands started to march down it. They were in tears as they tried to explain the impact of such a sight. As I waited for the parade to wind up at Grant Park I kept asking the policeman assigned to me how things were proceeding. At 2:30 in the afternoon he laughed and said people were still coming. And they kept coming. The final official city estimates were there were over two hundred thousand marchers and over three hundred thousand spectators. The police department reported that weekend had the lowest weekend crime rate they could remember.

I watched them as they marched into Grant Park, black, white, brown, red and Asian. There were Americans, Australians, Koreans and Vietnamese. They were with their families, friends, old and new, arm-in-arm. They were crying and laughing through their tears. Men in fatigues several sizes too small and men in tailored business suits. They were there in all shapes and sizes and as I looked it occurred to me that the greatest thing about them was they were not alone.

The Friday concert was a success. It started to lag a little bit after the speeches but it regained momentum when a local rock band started playing classic rock music that got everyone singing and dancing. It built to a full crescendo when Dennis took the stage. One hundred thousand people stood shouting and cheering before the Petrillo Band Shell as Dennis performed the hits he had written and performed while he was with Styx and the place came apart as he sang his new release, "Black Wall".

Although I did not march in the parade, I was content. This was my gift to these heroes and their families. Perhaps it would assuage some of the guilt I felt for leaving my post early. Being a part of "The Chicago Vietnam Veterans Welcome Home Parade" was one of the greatest moments of my life. I would like to be able to take some credit for its success but it's more than modesty or false humility that prohibits me from doing so. This was an event whose time had come. One of those movements that, once started, has a momentum all its own. As I think back on some of the mistakes we made and lack of experience in putting together anything near this magnitude I am convinced we couldn't have screwed this up even if we tried. We all worked hard but there was only one man who believed it would turn out as successful as it had.

Tom Stack died of cancer several years after the parade. Many believed it was due to his exposure to Agent Orange when he was in Vietnam. Tom struggled with his disease before, during and after the parade, but I never once heard any bitterness pass his lips.

After the parade, there was a true sea change in how the public in general viewed Vietnam veterans and how we viewed the public in return. In 1972, a year when America was still at war in Vietnam, a nationwide Harris Poll indicated that forty-nine percent of all Americans thought Vietnam veterans were "suckers", having to risk their lives in the wrong war. A follow-up poll in 1979 by the same organization indicated the number of Americans who thought the veterans were "suckers" had grown to sixty-four percent, a testament to the fact we had retreated and allowed our detractors to define us. After the parade, and to this day, all veterans are considered to be a respected and honored segment of our society. It's hard to determine, however, which came first. Did the parade actually change the consciousness of a nation, or was it the passing of time that softened the positions of both sides? Was the parade the final healing instrument or was it just the celebration of a fait accompli?

    I believe the parade was a unique experience touching both marchers and spectators in a highly individual way. For me it was an exhilarating release of suppressed emotions. By unlocking and freeing the demons I thought I had successfully and cleverly buried, my life took on a new genesis. I found it easier to talk about the war, and to my surprise, I found people who were actually interested in hearing about it. Not just to criticize and condemn, but to learn what it was like and why I thought it was important.

    I felt as though an enormous burden was lifted from my soul. My professional as well as my personal life soared. I was like the true believer, exalted after baptism, feeling reborn. Sadness, survivor guilt and despair that had been my unwelcome companions for so long were beginning to be exorcised. That doesn't mean the war or the memories are gone. They will be with me for the rest of my life. But the parade helped me to deal with my feelings in a more positive way.

Hundreds of veterans and spectators wrote to the Chicago newspapers and the parade office expressing their feelings about the parade. The following are representative of those letters. The first one is from a veteran who marched and the second one is from a spectator:

Mt. Pleasant, Ia:

"It's been some time since I left the greatest people and city in the world, Chicago. I'm still on an emotional high brought on by the Chicago Vietnam Vets Parade and welcome home celebration. Chicago, you've changed my life and I love you for it. As I sit here writing this, the feeling grows stronger – a feeling I can only describe as being in love.

Butterflies in my guts and apprehension in my soul were the prevalent feelings I experienced as I neared the loop. The minute after I pulled into the Americana Congress Hotel, those feelings left forever. "How long you stayin'?" the parking lot attendant asked. "At least two or three days," I replied. "You here for the parade?" "Yeah, I've waited a long time for this," I said. "What outfit you serve with in Nam?" he asked. I answered, "3rd Marine Division, 5th Comm. Battalion 1965-66." "Welcome home, sir, welcome home," he stated.

From that moment on I knew I was truly home. After twenty years of brooding and feeling sorry for us all, I felt vindicated. Those two words "Welcome Home" were magic, pure magic. I found two old buddies I'd served with in Nam, met many more "new" buddies and shared some very tender moments.

But the strangest thing of all was the fact that for the first time in over twenty years, I slept all night. To march in the parade was beyond all description. To all the people who lined the streets, hugged me, shook my hand and gave me back a part of myself I thought I'd left back in the jungles, I say thank you, from the bottom of my heart.

I love you and I can't wait to see you again. I'll come back as often as I am able.

D.D.

Oak Park, IL:

This day was paid for. You could see it in every face. They marched with such pride. One soldier walked out of his group and came over to shake my hand. I gave him the biggest grip I had.

They had come from everywhere for this day. It was rightfully theirs and no one was going to cheat them out of this little piece of appreciation that was so long overdue.

People clapped. Some held placards that said "THANKS" One young soldier climbed down from a truck and went over to give a beautiful young woman a kiss. The others in the truck cheered, the girl blushed and the crowd smiled some more.

They were wave after wave of fatigue uniforms in all shapes and sizes. Tanned, full of tattoos, shouting, marching cadences, drinking beer, all full with pride and relief. It was sweet, sweet, sweet, this hour of recognition. Still they came. Wave after wave. Crutches, wheelchairs, some strong straight men. They loved and we finally loved them back.

God forgive the foolish people who were so self-righteous in their hate for the war that they misplaced their humanity and withheld payment.

My dear, young, beautiful men who gave so much for so little, I hope with all my heart that last Friday helped.

W.S.

I received notices from veterans across the country that reunions were being planned for units reunited that weekend in Chicago. The seeds had been planted and were spreading and taking root. I think it will be a long time before the United States service men and women will be as disrespected as we were. That's not to say the true hardcore America haters won't spread their bile. The truth is, though, that they are small in number and hate everything about America.

Thanks Tom for believing this could happen and for allowing me to be a part of it. I'll see you after.

The End

THE WHITE HOUSE

WASHINGTON

May 8, 1986

I am honored to send warm greetings to everyone gathered for the "Welcome Home" Parade for Vietnam Veterans in Chicago.

We owe an everlasting debt of gratitude to our Vietnam Veterans. These courageous Americans never hesitated when our beloved nation called. Their sacrifices in Indochina have only recently received just recognition and praise. Your tribute is a wonderful example of how we can let them know that we shall never forget them or their fallen comrades-in-arms. On behalf of all Americans, I proudly join the people of Chicago in thanking and saluting our nation's Vietnam Veterans. God bless them, and God bless America.

Ronald Reagan

OFFICE OF THE MAYOR
CITY OF CHICAGO

HAROLD WASHINGTON
MAYOR

May 19, 1986

Dear Friends:

As Mayor of the City of Chicago, it is my extreme pleasure to join you for the Vietnam Veterans "Welcome Home" parade and activities.

I am proud to join the Chicago Veterans parade committee and the Citizens of Chicago for this long overdue "Welcome Home" celebration. We are all grateful for the Vietnam Veterans' outstanding contributions to our country.

We unite at this event to project to the world the true positive image of the Vietnam Veteran as well as an awareness of the pressing needs of veterans such as employment, and the POW/MIA and Agent Orange issues.

I wholeheartedly encourage all Chicagoans to gather on this Flag Day weekend and say thank you to the men and women of Vietnam for the great sacrifices made for our country.

Sincerely,

Harold W Washington

Mayor

Front- Bob Weiland, Man in uniform- General Westmoreland, Man to his left- Tom Stack, Man in wheel chair- James Partridge

Photographer: Tom Conroy

Chicago Tribune file photo. All rights reserved.
Used with permission. Staff Photo

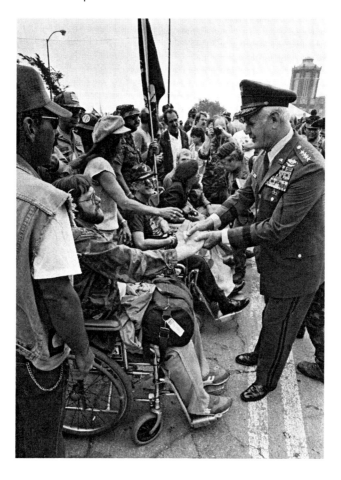

Chicago Tribune file photo. All rights reserved. Used with permission. Staff Photo

Chicago Tribune file photo. All rights reserved. Used with permission.

Photographer: Anne Cusack

Welcome Home

Chicago Tribune file photo. All rights reserved. Used with permission.

Photographer: Jerry Tomaselli

Chicago Tribune file photo. All rights reserved. Used with permission.

Photographer: Walter Kale

Chicago Tribune file photo. All rights reserved. Used with permission. Staff Photo

Hard Hats salute vets.

Chicago Tribune file photo. All rights reserved. Used with permission.

Photographer: Val Mazzenga

L-R: Tom Stack on Microphone, Gen. Westmoreland, Former Chicago Mayor Harold Washington.

Chicago Tribune file photo. All rights reserved. Used with permission.

Photographer: Walter Kale

Chicago Tribune file photo. All rights reserved. Used with permission.

Photographer: Phil Greer

Chicago Tribune file photo. All rights reserved. Used with permission.

Photographer: Jose More

Chicago Tribune file photo. All rights reserved. Used with permission.

Photographer: Jose More

Veteran in front of "Moving Wall"

By virtue of the authority vested in me as President of the United States and as Commander-in-Chief of the Armed Forces of the United States, I have today awarded

THE PRESIDENTIAL UNIT CITATION (NAVY)

FOR EXTRAORDINARY HEROISM TO

FIRST MARINE DIVISION (REINFORCED), FLEET MARINE FORCE

    For extraordinary heroism and outstanding performance of duty in action against enemy forces in the Republic of Vietnam from 16 September 1967 to 31 October 1968. Operating primarily in Quang Nam Province, the First Marine Division (Reinforced) superbly executed its threefold mission of searching for and destroying the enemy, defending key airfields and lines of communication, and conducting a pacification and revolutionary development program unparalleled in the annals of warfare. With the Division responsible for over 1,000 square miles of territory, it extended protection and pacification to more than one million Vietnamese. The countless examples of courage, resourcefulness, and dedication demonstrated by the officers and men of the First Marine Division attest to their professionalism and esprit de corps. Their combat activities were skillfully carried out in the face of adverse weather and difficult terrain such as canopied jungles, rugged mountains, swampy lowlands, and hot, sandy beaches. During the enemy Tet-offensive in late January of 1968, the First Marine Division dealt a devastating blow to enemy forces attempting to attack Danang. Again, in May 1968, the Division totally crushed an enemy drive directed against the Danang area through the Go Noi Island region southwest of Danang. The Division achieved this resounding victory through the skillful coordination of ground forces, supporting arms, and aircraft support. Most action in the I Corps Tactical Zone during August of 1968 was centered in the First Marine Division's tactical area of responsibility. The enemy, now looking for a victory which would achieve some measure of psychological or propaganda value, again mounted an attack of major proportions against Danang but were thoroughly repulsed, sustaining heavy casualties. The valiant fighting spirit, perseverance, and teamwork displayed by First Marine Division personnel throughout this period reflected great credit upon themselves and the Marine Corps, and were in keeping with the highest traditions of the United States Naval Service.

EPILOGUE

My life has been filled with great highs and deep lows as most lives have been . Some people close to me have asked how I can retain a positive outlook on life. I hope some of the answers are revealed in this book. The best news is that I'm alive. I live in the greatest country on the face of the earth, a country that allowed someone with my background to become successful in doing what I loved, the way I wanted to do it.My children, grandchildren, sisters and best friend all live within twenty-five minutes of my home and I see them often. I have wonderful memories of accomplishments and happiness. I have witnessed firsthand some of the historical events of my time and actively participated in them.

Despite the negative things that have happened to me I look back and realize I achieved many goals I had set for myself. In business, I have received awards, accolades and ample compensation for my efforts. In the arts, I have earned a Gold Album for my song writing. I am privileged to have been involved in humanitarian issues that I believe have made a difference like the parade and brining services to homeless veterans. And above all I am honored to have had the opportunity to serve my country as a United States Marine.

I have experienced many angels who have entered and exited my life. My daughter Lisa who selflessly out of love donated her kidney to save my life. My wife, who fought for me during the times when I was ready to give up. My daughters, who kept me occupied and busy with their company, their love, and by sharing their children. My sisters, who gave me their constant love, compassion and support. Dennis, who believed in my abilities to write and showing me that success is not limited to those from privileged backgrounds.

There was the naval doctor in Dodge City on that hellish day in 1968 who appeared from nowhere to save my arm. There are a myriad of other angels who, as health care providers, have helped me through all my injuries and illnesses from Vietnam to Japan, Glenview Naval Hospital in Illinois, VA Lakeside in Chicago, Hines VA in Maywood Illinois, Northwestern Memorial Hospital in Chicago and Silver Cross and Saint Joseph hospitals, both in Joliet, Illinois.

There are obviously too many names to remember but here are a few: Doctor Frederick Alexander who I consider to be as much a friend as a physician, Doctors Nahlia Ahmed, Nagarkatte, Kravetts, Dawson, Leventhal, Altergott, Georgheotti, Issa, Pettigrew and Narula. In addition, physical therapist Robert Bajt and the dialysis team at Silver Cross West in Joliet.

There is a sales closing technique that I learned early in my career. It is called the "Ben

Franklin Close". The idea is to draw a large "T" on a sheet of paper. On the left side above the top of the horizontal line you write the word "Pros". On the right side above the top of the horizontal line you write the word, "Cons." Then while using the vertical line to separate your responses you list the benefits of your products/services under these two. The idea is to be able to show that the pros far outweigh the cons, convincing the prospective client they will benefit from your offer. In applying this technique to my life I could come up with no other conclusion than I have been truly blessed.

I've come to believe strongly in these words:

"The longer I live, the more I realize the impact of attitude on life. Attitude, to me is
more important than facts. It is more important than the past, than education, than money, than circumstances, than failures, than successes, than what people think or say or do.

It is more important than appearance, giftedness or skill.

It will make or break a company…a church…a home.

The remarkable thing is that we have a choice every day regarding the attitude we will embrace for that day.

We cannot change our past…we cannot change the inevitable. The only thing we can do is play on the one string we have and that is our attitude.

I am convinced that life is ten percent what happens to me and ninety percent how I react to it.

And so it is with you. You are in charge of your attitudes."

Charles Swindoll

All in all life is good. There are helpful angels everywhere to assist you. All you need do is look for them.

Besides, how bad can things get?

What can they do to you? Send you to Vietnam?

CHICAGO VIETNAM VETERANS PARADE COMMITTEE, 1986

Honorary Chairman	Mayor Harold Washington
Chairman	Tom Stack
Vice Chairmen	William Davis Constance Edwards Phillip Meyer Col. Kenneth Plummer

Executive Committees:

Blinded Veterans	George Brummel
Business Liaison	William Horine
Communications/ Media	Bob Leonard
Counsel	Nealis, Bradley & Connell
Disabled Veterans	Doug Stout
Distribution Out of State Liaison	Linda Gonzales
Finance	Chuck Fabing
Medal of Honor	Sammy Davis Carmel Harvey Family (Posthumous) Allen Lynch Milton Olive III Family (Posthumous) Ken Stumps

Office manager	Jeff Harvey
POW/MIA	Mary Carol Lemon
Treasurer	Karen Harvey

Standing Committees:

Communications	John Wright
Community/Volunteer Outreach	Julio Gonzales
Fund Raising	Larry Langowski
Hospitality	Angelo Terrell
Program	Roger McGill

ADVISORY BOARD COMMITTEE

Dr. Alfonso Batres	Disabled American Veterans
Harold Blechman	
Jim Cepican	Veterans of Foreign Wars
Thomas C. Corcoran	National Restaurant Assoc.
Jim McElveen	Diederichs & Associates
William Dolan	Military Order of the Purple Heart
Brian Duffy	Windy City Veterans
Diane Carlson Evans	Vietnam Women's Memorial
John R. Fears	VA Edward Hines, Jr. Hospital

Simeon Fleming	Office of State Guardian
Robert Hanley	Chicago Police Marines
Thomas Har	Citicorp
Joe Hertel	Vietnam Veterans of America
Eric Johnson	Post Office
Herb Johnson	Combined Veterans
Irv Kupcinet	Chicago Sun-Times
Christopher Lane	Vet Center
Ray Laurence	Incarcerated Vets
Charles Lofrano	Automatic Data Processing
Faite Mack	
John Mahoney	American Legion
Joseph Mannion	Catholic war Veterans
Robert Mitchier	Navy Club of the United States
Tom Morgan	Veterans of Foreign Wars
Herman Herbert Moses	Jewish War Veterans
Ray Ney	Cmdr., Marine Corps League
Mickey O'Neill	American Ex-POWS
Samuel L. Parks	Vets Employment and Training
A.S. Pate	VA Edward Hines Jr. Hospital
Lee Perry	Air National Guard
Ed Rogers	VietNow
Scott Samuels	Chicago Convention and Visitors Bureau
Bob Scherbaum	Staley's Restaurant

Reggie Smith	Vets Assistance Commission
Paul Stanford, Jr.	VA Medical Center Director
John Steer	Minister
Ernest Stetz	Polish Legion of American Vets
Ray Sullivan	Military Order of the Purple Heart
Barry Summers	Vietnam Veterans of America
Lam Ton	South Vietnamese
Carmen Trombetta	Italian American War Veterans
Walter "Gibby" Vartan	Brig. General USAFR
Bob Gibson	Australian Vets
Col. Frank Marchant	

In addition to these names are hundreds of others who volunteered their time and energy to make the parade the largest of its kind in the history of the United States.

ABOUT THE AUTHOR

Charles S. Lofrano

Born on the far south side of Chicago.

Served in combat in Vietnam in 1968 as an M60 infantry machine gunner with 3rd Battalion, 27th Marines and 3rd Battalion, 7th Marines. Received a disabling gun shot wound and was decorated eight times.

One of the organizers of the Vietnam Veterans Welcome Home Parade in Chicago in 1986 that drew over 500,000 marchers and spectators.

Produced fund raising events for veterans with such artists as: Dennis De Young, Frankie Valli, Roy Clark, Rich Little, Danny Gans, and Linda Eder. Helped organize and sponsor 'Operation Stand Down" which brought services and resources to homeless veterans. National member of the VFW.

Song writer and recipient of a Gold album.

Survivor of organ failure, kidney dialysis for three and one half years, kidney transplant, four heart attacks and quadruple by pass surgery.

Thirty year career in the Information Technology Industry. Retired and currently residing in Illinois with wife of thirty eight years.

Made in the USA